Self-Coaching
for
Leaders

The unique and simple
approach to living
your personal and
professional dreams

Andrew Tallents

R^ethink

This book is dedicated to those that know me the best, those that have given me joy over the years and supported me in whatever I have chosen to do with my life. To my wife, Carolyn, for being the best example of a self-leader in action and for teaching me what being a family is all about; my three children, Beth, Harry and Sophie for showing me that anything is possible through hard work, passion, commitment and unconditional love; and my dad, mum and brother for helping to shape me into who I am today.

I would like to also dedicate this book to Peter Lever, for believing in me and investing in me during our time working together. It was a pivotal moment in my life. Finally, and perhaps most importantly, I would like to dedicate this book to those from disadvantaged backgrounds who have the potential, determination, ambition and discipline to remember their childhood dreams and become the leaders of tomorrow.

Contents

Foreword

How do the leaders of today achieve triple bottom-line performance without sacrificing environmental and social needs, not to mention their own personal dreams? This is a question that is increasingly front of mind as leaders grapple with the new challenges created by a different breed of stake-holders, who are more aware than ever that people and the planet need to also benefit when wealth is generated by businesses.

I first met Andrew when I was thinking about my own career transition from executive to non-executive life about fifteen years ago. He had been advising leaders like me for many years and understood the challenges of moving from executive life to a portfolio career. Subsequently, we worked together on leadership challenges faced by my portfolio organisations. Andrew always focused on trying to connect with the authenticity of the leaders he met to try and determine their chances of success in their personal and professional lives.

During the time that I have developed my non-executive portfolio, the world has changed beyond recognition in terms of how technology has enabled leaders to be more productive and seemingly always on call to serve the demands of their businesses. Leaders are under increasing pressure to deliver against short-term objectives with fewer resources and shorter investment cycles.

The Covid pandemic jolted the world into wondering whether there was another way. Young adults have tasted the benefits of working from home and will demand more flexible working in the future. Leaders are going to be facing different kinds of challenges as they engage their remote working teams and remote stakeholders. It could be argued that now is the opportunity for leaders to find a different way to live their complex and busy lives, but how do leaders successfully change their behaviours and habits over time?

I have been a great supporter of coaching and coaching cultures during my varied international career. I have seen leaders and their teams flourish when they show the courage to look deep within themselves to find the resources and potential that all human beings possess. Coaching has become more mainstream in organisations in the last decade and there is no longer a stigma attached to working with an executive coach. In my experience, the secret to sustainable leadership development is not purely in the coaching, but how the leader learns to self-coach when the coach is no longer in the room.

You may be reading this book as you can relate to the type of leaders many of us see: ambitious and success-ful to the outside world, but inside, they feel empty and unfulfilled. You may be reading this book because you have benefited from personal development ear-lier in your career, but more recently, have neglected this important aspect of self-actualisation. You may have recently reflected more often than in the past about who you are and why you are here.

Whatever the reason you are reading right now, I know that this book can help to support you to lead the life you truly deserve with twelve simple steps. Although the steps are simple, they are not easy to achieve. Andrew has developed pragmatic approaches drawn from his twenty-five years' experience of working with leaders like you, not only to explain the benefits of self-coaching, but ways to practise it successfully for the rest of your life.

During the time I have known Andrew, he has been able to bring a pragmatic approach to the way that leaders can become more self-aware of how to lead themselves to live their professional and personal dreams, while still delivering against their challenging business performance objectives.

This book summarises the approach Andrew takes with his clients as he supports them in being able to live their personal and professional dreams. I particularly like the snapshots of Amy as she develops in her new role. The summary of Amy's actions at the end of each chapter will encourage you to become action-oriented yourself.

I am proud to write the foreword for this book as I know and understand the genuine reasons that Andrew has written it. His purpose in life is to enable as many leaders as possible around the world to live their personal and professional dreams, while still making a difference to the planet they inhabit.

I hope you are inspired to be your true self, find your purpose in life and focus on what it is you are here to do. As Andrew regularly points out, the only person stopping you living your dreams each day is you.

Vanda Murray OBE DBA
Chair of Marshalls plc; Chair of Yorkshire Water; Senior Independent Director and Chair of Remuneration Committee of Bunzl plc; and Non-Executive Director and Chair of Remuneration and CSR Committees of Manchester Airport Group

Introduction

Since the year 2000, most leaders I have come across have grappled with two key questions: how do I achieve the short-term profit goals set by my shareholders, and how do I do this while pursuing my own personal dreams? I have worked closely with thousands of leaders over the last twenty years. Most of them focused on answering the first question and neglected the second question for most of their careers.

Those leaders who are curious and still have an appetite to learn more about how they can change their attitudes and behaviours to fulfil their potential while living their personal dreams have probably considered working with an executive or life coach at some point in their career. If they have chosen to work with a coach, they have probably improved their executive performance and/or become clearer about how they can work towards their personal dreams.

Leaders are increasingly experiencing new demands on their capabilities. Stakeholders are asking searching questions about how leaders are looking after their employees' wellbeing; they are asking how leaders are setting and meeting sustainability goals to support local and global communities during climate change. Leaders are also being asked to meet both short- and long-term profit targets. Sustainable long-term wealth creation will become increasingly important in the coming years. These extra demands tend to amplify the focus on meeting leaders' professional goals and make their personal goals seem impossible to reach.

Since the Covid pandemic, something has shifted in the way many leaders view their lives. It has raised questions like, 'Who am I?', 'Why am I here?' and, 'What am I doing?' Such questions can lead to many people feeling lost and wondering what they should do next in their busy and complex lives. Leaders now need a different kind of support from their coaches. In the past, ambitious leaders engaged executive or life coaches to help them succeed in their professional and personal lives, but many coaches used their significant business and life experience to mentor their clients rather than coach them. They were directive and solution-oriented. Leaders became dependent on the coaches, so once the coaches left the relationship, the leaders tended to revert back to their old ways of working.

In the twenty years I have been working with leaders, my experience is that many find it incredibly difficult to self-coach effectively. They usually sacrifice their personal dreams to deliver against their professional goals, and resentment and frustration build up over time. The biggest mistake leaders make is thinking that they have to be like someone else to achieve their personal and professional dreams. They believe they aren't good enough to realise those dreams and that they have to rely on others and the right circumstances to achieve them rather than making it happen themselves.

Most leaders need someone to challenge their thinking and help them recognise why they are sacrificing personal dreams in favour of achieving their professional dreams. Executive and life coaching on their own no longer provide what leaders really need. Leaders need to be coached in the short term, but more importantly, supported to learn how to self-coach themselves every day in order to be able to truly live their personal and professional dreams in the long term. My coaching approach with leaders focuses on the coaching they need, but also teaches them how to self-coach after our sessions have finished. This is the type of coaching that most leaders will need in the coming years.

This book is the product of many conversations and observations that I have developed into a framework of twelve disciplines that any leader can develop over time to help them move closer to living their dreams. The self-coaching framework provided in this book uses the most pragmatic aspects of coaching to create insight for the leader, but also teaches them how to self-coach when a coach is not available to them.

The book is useful both for leaders that have experience of working with coaches and those that have never worked with a coach before. It draws on my personal experience of coaching and being coached, and also ideas and models from other thought leaders and authors that have helped me on my self-coaching journey. My unique twelve-discipline model differs from others in that you take control of the direction of your own life and learn how to coach yourself rather than relying on other people to lead you to your dreams. The steps are easy to follow and pragmatic in their approach. You can learn and practise the steps at your own pace and can choose what help you might need from friends, associates and professionals as you progress through the book.

Self-coaching can be simply defined as the process of leading your own personal development, through self-leadership and the support of others, to help maximise your personal and professional potential.

It is important to note that you lead your own personal development, but *with the support of others*. Self-coaching is rarely successful when pursued alone. It is also a cyclical process. As you coach yourself to move closer to your dreams, you become more self-aware of other ways you can help yourself.

Every leader is unique and will be at different stages of their self-coaching journey. Leaders are generally in one of three stages of the self-coaching cycle: **Reconnect**, **Refocus** or **Regenerate**. Many are in the Reconnect stage of the cycle and some are in the Refocus stage, but few are within the Regenerate stage.

The self-coaching cycle

The self-coaching cycle

The book is divided into three parts: one for each of the stages of the self-coaching cycle. Although it is preferable to read the book from start to finish, some leaders may choose to dive right into the chapters that explain the stage that resonates with them most. Each chapter starts with a short 'fly on the wall' account of Amy, a newly-appointed leader, as she navigates what many leaders experience as they develop each discipline of their self-coaching journey. This is followed by a detailed description of the discipline itself. The end of each chapter provides actions that will help leaders apply the learning to their own personal situation and an opportunity to read Amy's actions so that leaders can gain some insight into how others use the content to self-coach.

Once you have read the book, you should better understand who you are and have discovered a variety of ways to be your authentic self while achieving your personal and professional dreams. This will ensure you become more authentic as a leader and build stronger relationships with many of your key stakeholders. You will be focused on achieving the essential things that need to get done as you work towards your dreams, and will learn how to coach yourself back on track when you feel you are moving away from the path that you have decided is your destiny.

PART ONE
RECONNECT

1
Self-Leadership

Amy looked at herself in the mirror. Today was the first day of the rest of her life. She had managed to secure the biggest job in her career to date. She was joining Fortune Industries as Chief Operating Officer and was feeling both excited and nervous about the opportunities the role presented. Excited, as this was a chance to prove herself at board level, but nervous, as her five previous promotions at Fortune's major competitor had been heavily sponsored by her long-term boss. Could she make it on her own in a new culture with her new boss, Carlos?

At the board's suggestion, Amy had employed an experienced executive coach to help her with her onboarding. Her first session had taken place the previous week. Amy had never had coaching before, and she was pondering on something the coach had asked her as she made her way to the office. How could she use the discipline of self-leadership to ensure that her first ninety days at Fortune would make the maximum impact in her role? Amy understood the theory. Today, she was going to be tested on how it worked in practice.

December 1984: India was in a state of transition after the murder of Indira Gandhi; 'Do They Know It's Christmas?' was the Christmas number one in the UK; the first Apple Macs were on sale and Ronald Reagan was re-elected as president of the United States of America. I was fifteen years old and living in Macclesfield, Cheshire in the UK. My dad was working in Saudi Arabia, my mum was suffering serious health problems and my younger brother was struggling with my dad being away for long periods of time.

I was excited that my dad had invited us all to Jedda for Christmas. What should have been an exciting adventure soon became a sudden realisation of my coming of age. During the trip, my dad confided in me how big the problems were with my mum and brother and asked for my help in supporting them while he was away. I came home, took my mock high school exams, and the results made me realise that I needed to completely rethink the way I lived my life. It was my first experience of being forced to develop self-leadership as a discipline.

Self-leadership can be defined as the intentional influencing of the way we think, feel and behave to achieve our personal and professional goals in life.

In reality, many people only practise self-leadership when a life-changing event happens to them and they need to react in some way and take control of the situation. We can all think of friends and family who have displayed courage and tenacity to get themselves out of difficult situations, but in everyday life some of us tend to put up with the status quo as there is no burning platform forcing us to act.

To bring self-leadership to life, consider the analogy that Andrew Bryant uses in his book *Self-Leadership: How to become a more successful, efficient, and effective leader from the inside out*.[1] Think about the key relationships in your life, particularly about one that maybe isn't where you want it to be at the moment. It may be with:

- Your partner
- Your parents
- Your sibling/s
- Your team
- Your organisation
- Your boss
- Your friend/s
- Yourself

---

1   A Bryant, *Self-leadership: How to become a more successful, efficient, and effective leader from the inside out* (McGraw-Hill Education, 2012)

SELF-COACHING FOR LEADERS

Imagine yourself driving in a sports car on a steep and dangerous mountain road in the Swiss Alps with the person you want to have a better relationship with. You are in the passenger seat and the other person is in the driver's seat. The driver of the vehicle is in charge of the speed that you go, how you take the corners and generally how comfortable they make you feel in your driving experience together. If you find that you become a backseat driver, complaining and becoming judgmental about how the driver is making you feel, then it's probably time that you consider exercising self-leadership in the relationship. This is the time that you should work with the other person to decide when it is your turn to sit in the driver's seat.

Although the definition of self-leadership is clear, the way in which it is practised is about understanding who you are and how you behave, and then deciding to change that behaviour with intent, to enable you to fulfil your potential as a human being. You need to be responsible for your own thoughts, feelings, speech and behaviour. You need to be responsible for the commitments you make to yourself and others. You are not responsible for the way other people behave, think or feel.

Now think about the people you normally interact with week to week. Can you think of anyone who tends to moan about their personal situation and blames others for what is happening to them in their own lives? Perhaps someone who you think should stop playing the victim and should just get off their backside and do something about their own personal situation?

Now think about some of the people that you trust the most in your lives. Try and think whether, during the last few months, they may have been thinking or saying the same thing about you. Perhaps they believe you should stop playing the victim and start to exert more influence in changing the situation you find yourself in? Raising self-awareness about who is in the driver's seat in your key relationships is the first step in practising self-leadership.

The Wheel of Life

The original concept of The Wheel of Life is attributed to the late Paul J Meyer who founded the Success Motivation Institute® in 1960.[2] It is another useful tool to enable you to think about whether you are adopting self-leadership in important aspects of your life.

You can design your own wheel of life or use the example wheel below. The ten 'spokes' of the wheel represent the various roles in your life.

---

2   https://pauljmeyer.com/the-legacy/industry-pioneer

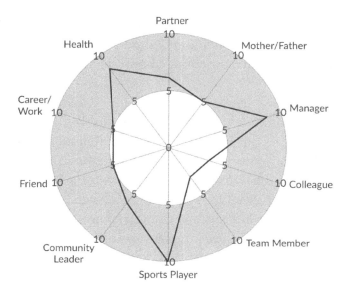

The Wheel of Life[3]

Some questions to consider when looking at this diagram that can provide insight into the balance in your life include:

- How are you looking after your mental wellbeing and your personal development?

- How are you looking after your physical wellbeing?

- How are you engaging with society and culture in your life?

- What is important to you spiritually, and what ethics are important to you?

3   Adapted from Paul J Meyer's Wheel of Life, www.pauljmeyer.com

- Where do you sit in relation to your role in your family at home?

- How are you managing your finances and your career goals?

- How much quality time are you spending with your friends?

- Are you in the driving seat in these areas or are others in your life deciding where you are focusing your time?

Once you have given serious thought about where you are spending your time, give yourself a score between 1 and 10 for each role depending on how happy you are with the self-leadership role you are playing. A score of 1 would indicate that you are completely dissatisfied with how you are fulfilling your role and a score of 10 would indicate you are content with how you are fulfilling your role. Once you have plotted your scores on each spoke of the wheel, join the dots to form a spiderweb diagram like the one above. This will help you assess where you might be out of balance.

Benefits of practising self-leadership

In a recent survey of global leaders undertaken by the Tallents Partnership, 53% of respondents stated that they did not view themselves as effective self-leaders. Indeed, only 5% of leaders stated that they were extremely effective in the discipline of self-leadership.[4] This is not uncommon. Those leaders who have chosen to practise self-leadership in their own lives have seen big improvements in these areas:

- More self-awareness about who they are and how their behaviours affect their own feelings and those around them.

- More self-confidence in their ability to be in charge of their own lives and work towards their goals.

- Better understanding of their purpose in life, why they are here and who they serve.

- Decreased stress and anxiety due to being more accepting of what they can and can't control in their lives.

- Increased happiness due to feeling more fulfilled in their lives and positive about their relationships.

- Deeper relationships due to the fact they are authentic, trustworthy and vulnerable in the way they live their lives.

Making decisions to lead our own lives is not easy for many of us. We have a fear of making the wrong decisions and so we miss opportunities and assess risks incorrectly. We don't think we have permission to say no to people, even where we know the action does

---

4   Tallents Partnership Leadership Survey (April 2021)

not serve us on our own journey. We also don't think we have the right to say yes to what is important to us as we are often thinking about others first. Asking for help from others or showing enough vulnerability to make others aware of our weaknesses is also difficult. We are hardwired from childhood in the way we make decisions. This is partly due to nature, but also the environments in which we have grown up.

Karpman's Drama Triangle

An interesting model that can help and support us in becoming self-leaders is Stephen B. Karpman's Drama Triangle.[5]

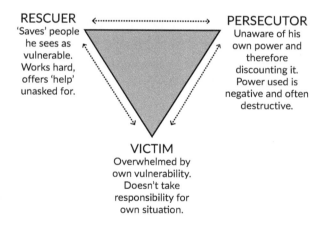

RESCUER
'Saves' people he sees as vulnerable. Works hard, offers 'help' unasked for.

PERSECUTOR
Unaware of his own power and therefore discounting it. Power used is negative and often destructive.

VICTIM
Overwhelmed by own vulnerability. Doesn't take responsibility for own situation.

Karpman's Drama Triangle

5   S Karpman, 'Fairy Tales and Script Drama Analysis', *Transactional Analysis Bulletin* 7(26), 1968

In any of our relationships, we tend to sit in one of three positions on the triangle at any time. The other person in the relationship sits in one of the other places. Here is a case study of how this works in our family.

My 14-year-old son has a certain amount of credits to use on an online game on his Xbox. I bought him the credits as a birthday gift on the understanding that he would not ask for any more when they ran out. However, when they did run out he came to ask me for more money to buy more credits.

I immediately took the position of persecutor and used my position of power to withhold funds and make him feel the consequences of his mistake. He then took the victim position in telling me it wasn't fair and that I was mean and didn't understand how important it was for him to be able to play the game. My wife then saw him in the victim position and felt that I had been unfair to him.

She felt sorry for him so gave him the opportunity to earn some more money by doing some jobs and, in doing so, took on the rescuer position with him and the persecutor position with me. As far as I was concerned this undermined my authority and I became the victim in the relationship with my wife, blaming her for not agreeing with my stance.

This is how the drama triangle unfolds in many family disputes. The drama triangle exists in many of our relationships, and learning the discipline of self-leadership can help us break free of the triangle. Take a moment to think about a drama triangle that exists in your relationships. Which of the three positions feels more comfortable for you to take?

David Emerald developed a concept called TED (The Empowerment Dynamic) as a means to break out of the drama triangle.[6] The diagram below shows that by becoming more self-aware about which position we are in, we can take a self-leadership approach to break free of the triangle and release the potential within ourselves and our relationships.

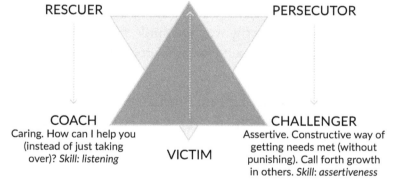

CREATOR
Accepting own vulnerability, realising they have power too, thinking about options. *Skill: problem-solving*

RESCUER   PERSECUTOR

COACH   CHALLENGER
Caring. How can I help you   Assertive. Constructive way of
(instead of just taking   getting needs met (without
over)? *Skill: listening*   VICTIM   punishing). Call forth growth
                                           in others. *Skill: assertiveness*

The Empowerment Triangle[7]

---

6   D Emerald, *The Power of TED: The Empowerment Dynamic* (Polaris Publishing, 2015)

7   Adapted from D Emerald, *The Power of TED: The Empowerment Dynamic*

- The persecutor can become the challenger by becoming more assertive.

- The rescuer can become the coach by being more caring and responding when help is really needed.

- The victim can become a creator by accepting their own vulnerability and realising that they have the power to solve their own problems.

Take a moment to think about how you can move to a better place in the triangle in a relationship that is tough at the moment.

Chapter summary

- Self-leadership can be defined as the intentional influencing of the way we think, feel and behave to achieve our personal and professional goals in life.

- Only 5% of leaders are effective in the discipline of self-leadership. By practising self-leadership, you can differentiate yourself as a leader.

- Practising self-leadership leads to improvements in personal and professional performance levels over time.

- You need to be responsible for your own thoughts, feelings, speech and behaviour.

- You need to be responsible to the commitments you make to yourself and others but you are not responsible for the way other people behave, think or feel.

- Don't wait for a life-changing event. Be proactive and try to practise self-leadership every day.

- Raise self-awareness about your behaviour in key relationships.

- The Wheel of Life can be a useful tool in helping you to work out where to focus your self-leadership energy.

- Use Karpman's Drama Triangle to help you set clear self-leadership goals in your key relationships.

- Get support from friends, mentors and coaches to hold you to account on every step of the self-leadership journey.

Actions

- Look at your key relationships. Are you the driver or the passenger?

- Create your own wheel of life. Are you leading a balanced life?

- Assess where you sit in the drama triangle of a relationship. Decide where you want to sit in the future.

- If you currently lead a team, rate your team's dysfunctionality on a scale of 1 to 10. (1 is completely functional and high-performing and 10 is completely dysfunctional. Most leaders tend to score between 5 and 10.)

- Ask yourself these questions:
  - How do I contribute to that dysfunctionality?
  - What behaviours of mine impact negatively on the team?
  - Using the discipline of self-leadership, what can I do tomorrow to enable the team to function more effectively and move the dysfunctionality score to a lower number?

- Think about one area of your personal or professional life where you can take the wheel and determine your direction in the coming weeks and months. Take a moment to commit to one small step forward and share that step with someone you trust.

Amy's actions

Action notes from coaching session

Self-leadership

I am prepared to lead myself.

I am the passenger in the relationships with my partner and Carlos.

The Wheel of Life taught me that I need to focus on my wellbeing and my friendships.

In the drama triangle I often sit in the persecutor position. I need to become more self-aware of how this damages my relationships.

Team dysfunctionality score is 7.
I contribute to this by not delegating effectively.

One step I can take tomorrow is to step back and listen more before acting and look for opportunities to trust more and delegate tasks.

2
Who Am I?

Amy referred to her action notes from her last coaching session and recognised that she was feeling more accountable for her own decisions. She had stopped blaming others for her mistakes and had identified where she wanted to go in her life.

At the start of her next session, Amy's coach asked: 'Who are you in your key relationships?' Amy was perplexed at first, but during the coaching session she gained insight into how many different versions of herself she was without even realising it. She had gained feedback from her new CEO that she didn't seem herself in important meetings. Amy realised that she needed to embark on a journey of self-discovery and understand who she really was so that she could stop trying to be somebody else.

What would your reply be if somebody asked you, 'Who are you?' Sometimes leaders are scared to answer this question. Sometimes they have never thought about the question before. Sometimes they think they are sure about the answer, but after exploring further, they realise they didn't know who they really were after all. This is both common and normal. We are so busy doing things that we don't make enough time to think deeply about who we are.

In the recent global leadership survey, we asked leaders how clear they were about who they really were and 33% of leaders stated that they were not clear.[8] This response surprised me a little, as normally many more leaders struggle with this question. Perhaps during the pandemic more leaders had taken time out to understand more about their own strengths and weaknesses and learn how they needed to adapt to their new environments, but the result still means that one in three leaders struggle with this question.

Why it is so important to know who we are

There have been many research studies over the last decade that show that the most effective leaders in the world are authentic. Authentic leaders:

- Understand who they are and they make every effort to reflect that every minute of the day

---

8   Tallents Partnership Leadership Survey (April 2021)

- Are aware of their strengths, limitations and emotions

- Create followership

- Choose to show their real selves to their followers

Of course, all of us have different roles to play in life. One of my clients discovered that she was different with every single person that she knew. The only person in her life that saw her authentic self was her husband. This is not uncommon, but it can be exhausting when you are trying to remember who you should be with the different people in your life. Coaching and self-coaching can help a leader to understand what support they might need to become more authentic.

Behaviour assessment

When we are interested in exploring who we are, it is useful to focus on our behaviours. There are many ways in which we can try and work out who we are by gaining insight into how we behave as humans. This isn't about personality; it's about our observable behaviours, which are a gateway to communication. When people observe our behaviour, we are either interacting with other people, or we are performing a task.

One reliable behaviour assessment tool that is simple to understand is DISC profiling. It was first proposed in 1928 by William M Marston, a physiological psychologist, in his book *Emotions of Normal People*.[9] In the DISC model, Marston lists four major aspects to our observable behaviour:

1. **D is for Dominance:** If I have this as a key characteristic of my behaviour, I tend to need control in my life. I need to dominate situations and I don't like people taking control of what I am doing. I tend to be more decisive and the loudest person in the room. If I have a low score in the dominance aspect, then I am more measured and I am more inclusive. I tend not to need to be the centre of attention and don't always need to be in control, so I've got a tendency to follow rather than lead. I also like to reflect on any decisions I need to make.

2. **I is for Influence:** This is about how much influence a person needs to have when interacting with others. If I have a high influence score, then I need to be around people. I need to chat with people to really engage and understand how they feel and I also make decisions through interacting with people. If I'm around people, I feel energised. If I have a low influence score, then I don't need people to be around me as much. I am content with my own company and I can happily work on my own. It doesn't mean I can't read people well and build relationships, but I don't need to have them around me all the time.

9   WM Marston, *Emotions of Normal People* (Franklin Classics, 2015)

3. **S is for Steadiness:** This is all about the pace and steadiness in which I deliver my work to a high-quality standard. A high steadiness score means that I need to deliver high standards in the quality of work I offer. I typically want to work at a slower pace (my pace). It's all about how I work. I am happy to work as part of a team. I will dot the i's and cross the t's and I will make sure that my work is completed on time. You know you can always rely on me to deliver what I agree to deliver. A low steadiness score means I tend to be a fire-starter. I will start lots of things and I will thrive on change. I need lots of variety. I won't be worried about the quality of my work as much and I will not need to feel part of a team as much. I am just as happy working on my own. I tend to be late for appointments and sometimes don't show up at all if the subject matter is not of interest to me.

4. **C is for Compliance:** This is all about following the rules. If I have a high compliance score, then I feel I have to follow the rules. I don't question them as every rule is there for a reason. It's a way of life because the rules provide order. I also make sure that others know how important the rules are and ensure that they follow them. I am a stickler for the rules. Indeed, if the rules are not clear or they aren't there at all, then I am the one that will create them and make sure everyone follows them. Lower compliance scores mean that I tend to be creative in my interpretation

of the rules. The rules are there to be bent and shaped and sometimes even broken. I will take more risks and don't need structure around me to succeed in life. I tend to be the change agent and will make the rules up as I go along to support the way things can get done in the most efficient way.

The composition of these four elements of behaviour varies for each leader. By understanding your own observable behaviours, you can become more aware of when they are helpful and when they are unhelpful. Take a few moments to make a note of how you might typically behave against the four aspects. Where are you high, low or in the middle? We tend to be higher in at least two of these aspects.

My two highest aspects are Influence and Dominance. I need to be around people and feel energised by working with other people. I need to be in control of my life and to feel like I am able to make decisions quickly and not have other people make decisions for me. These two aspects of my behaviour are important to me. Less important to me are the Steadiness and Compliance behaviour aspects. I need other people around me that can execute to a high standard and I like to work at a high pace and move on to the next thing before I finish the job I am working on today. I am someone who likes to bend the rules and form new rules so that they benefit the way I work.

Self-coaching is helpful when looking at my four behaviours and deciding whether I am able to behave in those ways in my day-to-day life. If I am able to, then I am living an authentic life. If I am not, then I am using energy to be someone other than myself, and this is exhausting over a long period of time.

Values

Eduard Spranger, a German psychologist, is regarded as the father of human values and motivations as he was the first psychologist to identify the true values of mankind.[10] We tend to think of values as things like honesty, timekeeping, friendliness or loyalty. For Spranger, those were virtues because that's how a person would behave 'in a virtuous way'.

The bigger question he had was 'why' they behaved in a virtuous way, and that journey led to his publication in 1928 called *Types Of Men: The psychology and ethics of personality*, which was the precursor to works we see today. Spranger's original book only listed six values, but work in the 1950s by Gordon Allport updated the values ranking and added a seventh value.[11] These were modernised further in the early 2000s by Gerry Donaldson, a physicist and founder of CCR3 Group, a firm developing AI around people performance

10   E Spranger, *Types of Men: The psychology and ethics of personality* (Niemeyer, 1928)
11   GW Allport, *The Nature of Prejudice* (Addison-Wesley, 1979)

where the true intent from Spranger was researched and again, brought up to date for the twenty-first century regarding meaning, terminology and intent.

Donaldson's values give leaders clear insight into what drives them on a daily basis. Of the seven values listed below you will have about three that tend to be motivators for you. These values drive your daily decision-making processes and associated behaviours.

1. **Aesthetic Value:** This is a value that drives for balance and harmony. If this is important to you and part of your value system then when you walk into a room, you'll be looking at how the light falls off the walls, where the natural light is coming into the room and how the furniture is positioned within the room. If it doesn't look right, you'll probably try and make it look better and balance the room in an organised way which makes sense to you. When leading teams, you will want to make sure that the team is well-balanced and there's harmony with little conflict.

2. **Altruistic Value:** If this is important to you, you will look to help others first. If you're a leader of a team then you'll be aware of how other people around you benefit from the decisions you make and will be evaluating how a decision can help the team members grow as human beings and how to help them fulfil their potential.

3. **Economic Value:** This is about two things: it can be a practical financial return for an individual, such as salary that's commensurate with their level and position, or it can be a heartfelt reputation for being successful. Sometimes it can be both. If this is important to you, then you will tend to make decisions that enable you to either gain more financial return or a reputation for being successful.

4. **Individualistic Value:** This value looks to identify the uniqueness in the person or things that make you stand out from the crowd. This is inherent in those who promote strong will and opinion when creating their own space. You will know the people that hold this value as they are always offering opinions, even when they're not asked for.

5. **Political Value:** This is not about being political as such. It is really about the value of power and control over one's own destiny. If this value is key to you, then when somebody tells you what to do, or other people affect your progress, there'll be a disconnect. This value looks to dominate all it surveys. Many CEOs have this as a key value.

6. **Theoretical Value:** This is about the drive for knowledge, learning and understanding. Knowledge is essential to being complete, so if you lose the ability to learn there is a disconnect

and you will seek other roles or projects where you can start to learn again.

7. **Traditional Value:** This value promotes a system for living one's life and to have rules by which you live your life. Standards, habits and routines, order and structure are what make the world go around. If you are in an environment where you can't create that structure, you'll feel that disconnect and something won't feel right until you feel part of a system again.

Take a few moments to write down what you think your top three values are. As you build your own self-awareness of who you really are, how you behave and what you value, you need to accept this and work out what is needed to support this authenticity every day. This is a choice. Developing who you really are takes patience, vulnerability, high levels of emotional intelligence and the practice of mindfulness. We will explore these concepts in later chapters.

Having access to and understanding DISC profiles provides you with choices in how to build relationships with stakeholders. How might you go about this? A self-coaching leader might decide to be open with stakeholders, asking them how they prefer to behave and what they really value. They could then come to an agreement with stakeholders on how they might work together effectively to keep as many elements of their natural behaviours as possible and stay true to their own values in their relationships.

The most important parts of this process in terms of self-coaching are vulnerability, holding each other to account in the relationship, using emotional intelligence in the moment to understand how you are behaving, and constantly asking for feedback. This is not easy to do, but it does enable you to self-coach and become even more self-aware about who you are in relationships.

You can easily access DISC assessments on the internet or contact the Tallents Partnership if you would like to learn more and access our bespoke DISC and VALUEMETRIC tools.

Chapter summary

- Understanding who you are is a deep and meaningful process. It is not a simple or quick exercise.

- At least 33% of leaders are not clear about who they really are.

- Authentic leaders understand who they are and that they create a followership.

- You can raise self-awareness about your behaviours and your values.

- Accepting who you are and being curious about how others are can strengthen key stakeholder relationships.

- It's valuable to ask for feedback on how you are doing in changing your behaviour to become more authentic, and how you are improving your effectiveness.

- You can determine who you want to be in the long term, and plan to change your behaviours over time.

Actions

- Ask yourself the question, 'Who am I?' Try to consider this for at least fifteen minutes and write something down that captures the essence of who you are.

- Think about the roles you play in life. How many of them are you being your true self in?

- Think about the DISC profile behaviours. What are your highest and lowest elements?

- Think about the seven values. What are your top three values?

- Assess your team members' behaviours and values. What does this tell you about how the team is functioning?

- Practise self-leadership and build your emotional intelligence by being aware of how you behave and what you value in key moments of your life.

- Ask for feedback when you start to change behaviours in key relationships to see how they're being received.

Amy's actions

Action notes from coaching session

Who am I?

I am not the same person in all my relationships. Carlos is right, I do pretend to be more senior in board meetings.

My DISC profiles taught me that I love being around people and I get things done. I reflect on decisions I need to make. I like to bend the rules a little.

My top three values are Economic, Individualistic and Political. I now understand why I make certain decisions.

I am going to assess my team and also ask Carlos to take the DISC & Values assessment so we can understand each other better.

3
Why Am I Here?

Amy was making good progress. She had been in her new role for three months and was feeling more authentic about how she engaged with others at work. She had discussed with Carlos how they could be more authentic in their relationship and she understood how to align her decision-making to her key economic, political and individualistic values. She had committed to only offering her opinions when they would add value to the situation. She had also become more self-aware of when her natural tendency to take control of situations was unhelpful.

Something was troubling her, though. In the pit of her stomach, she felt slightly disconnected from Fortune Industries' values and purpose. She decided to focus on this issue in the next session with her coach. She was asked to undertake several creative exercises and was pleased to rediscover what was important to her in her personal and professional life. She agreed with her coach that she

*would share this insight with her CEO and find a way to
weave her own purpose and values into those of the senior
leadership team.*

According to the Tallents Partnership global leadership survey, 50% of respondents stated that they were
not totally clear about their purpose in life.[12] Being
unclear about your purpose in life impacts both your
personal and professional goals.

Why leaders lose their way in life

The previous chapter discusses the importance of
understanding our value systems. Our three key
values get us out of bed in the morning and keep
us motivated in our leadership roles. If any one of
these three values cannot be realised in our current
leadership roles, then we can become demotivated
and disconnected from our roles in life. Likewise, if
the core purpose of the organisation we work for is
not clear, or becomes diluted compared to when we
joined, then we can also become disconnected from a
role without really understanding why.

Many of us have witnessed situations where leaders
have become extremely successful in their careers, but
wake up one day asking the question if it was really
worth all the sacrifices they made along the way.

---

12 Tallents Partnership Leadership Survey (April 2021)

Many successful leaders struggle in their marriages and don't have many hobbies outside of work. They don't keep in contact with their friends and family, and ultimately end up feeling that they are in a lonely place.

Once leaders achieve success and the financial rewards and lifestyle that comes with this, sometimes it can be difficult to risk losing what they already have. They choose to stay safe and comfortable in their current roles when they are really ready for their next challenge. They can become bored and feel trapped and lost in their own lives.

Some leaders who are successful in life choose to slow down. They create space and time to really think about the reasons they are doing what they are, and decide that they don't really know. Their career success has been driven through the expectations of others and they start to question the value of their personal success. They have lost their sense of purpose in life.

Why having purpose is so important for us

If we understand our purpose, we can focus on our short-term and long-term goals. My own purpose in life is to help as many influential leaders to fulfil their potential as human beings. My short-term goal is to help today's influential leaders learn about themselves and fulfil their leadership potential. My long-term goal is to work with young, future leaders to help them make a positive impact on the world. When anyone asks me to work with them, I ask myself the question, 'Will time spent with this person move me closer to these goals?' If it will, I spend time with them. If it won't, I refer them to someone else that can help them.

Purpose also enables us to prioritise our day-to-day activities and relationships. Being clear about our own purpose makes it clear about who we are in service of. In my case, I am in service of those influential leaders who want to learn more about how to fulfil their own potential. I should not be spending time with any other types of leaders.

Scientific research shows us that understanding our own purpose in life is a key ingredient in our ability to build our long-term resilience, recover quickly from setbacks and maintain our focus on what is important in challenging times.

Living a life full of purpose means when we get up each morning and look at ourselves in the mirror, we know that we are making a difference. We gain a sense of fulfilment and contentment from our actions. Even though I feel tired at the end of a full day of coaching, I know that I have done my best to help influential leaders to make their own difference in the world.

Self-coaching techniques to discover why you are here

These techniques will help you discover why you are here. The first will help you to work out the reasons why you are not feeling connected to your current roles in life. As humans, we have a natural affinity for helping others, so the second will support you to decide who you are in service of today, and who you would like to be of service to in the future. The third exercise enables you of decide what kind of legacy you would like to leave with the world once you have gone, and the last exercise uses creativity to help you define your true purpose in life and take the first steps towards living a purposeful life.

Technique 1: Energisers and drains

Take a few minutes to create two columns on a piece of paper. One column will be energisers and the other will be drains. Think about the role/s you have had in the last ten years and which aspects of the role/s energised and drained you. Make a list of each of them. The table below lists some of my energisers and drains.

Once you have your two lists, think about each energiser and drain in turn. If the energiser is present in your most recent role, put a tick next to it. If it isn't, then put a cross. If the drain is present in your most recent role, put a cross next to it. If it isn't, then put a tick.

Energisers	Drains
Learning	Politics
Walking	Time-wasters
Coaching	Victims
Debating	Bureaucracy
People	Administration
Travel	Laziness
Thinking of new ideas	Arrogance
Teaching	Egos
Writing	Jobsworths

Now count up the number of ticks and crosses in both columns. If the total number of ticks outweighs the crosses, then you should be feeling fairly content with the role you are in. If the number of crosses outweigh the ticks, then it may be time to think about changing the way you perform your role, and possibly the way you are living your life.

Technique 2: Who are you in service of?

This question reminds leaders that their self-development is not about them, but about the people that they are in service of. It helps to bring perspective when a leader feels lost or confused about purpose.

Take a couple of minutes to note down who you are in service of today, and who you would like to be in service of in the future. How does this resonate with what you are currently doing in your life?

Here are some of the people and groups that I am in service of.

Mother	Son	Daughters	Spouse
Business partners	Young adults	Community leaders	Sports team
Friends	Clients	Leaders	Colleagues

Technique 3: Legacy

In *The 7 Habits of Highly Effective People*, Stephen Covey asks you to reflect on what would you want mourners to be saying about you and your legacy if you were to attend your own funeral service as an invisible presence at the end of a long, purposeful and fulfilling life.[13]

Think deeply about this question for the next five minutes and jot down the words and sentences that come to mind. What would your family be saying about you? Your friends? Your work colleagues? What would those you had been in service of during your life be saying about you? Covey suggests that some people find real purpose in writing a full eulogy about their lives from the perspective of those that they have

---

13   S Covey, *The 7 Habits of Highly Effective People* (Simon & Schuster, 1999)

served. Some leaders choose to be more creative and write a poem that describes the rich life they have lived. Do what feels right for you.

Technique 4: Creative approach

An insight of what energises and drains you, who you would like to be in service of (now and in the future) and what kind of legacy you would like to leave behind when you are gone is really useful as you move into the final exercise. This focuses on bringing your purpose to life. You will need to spend between five and thirty minutes to complete this exercise, but it will be worth it.

Purpose question: If I had no limitations whatsoever, how would I choose to live my life over the next five years, using the experience and skills I have gained to date, in service of those I choose to serve?

Once you have this question written down, spend as much time as you need *drawing* your answer on an A4 piece of paper. You don't need to show your drawing to anybody, so don't worry if you are not a natural artist. What is important is that you draw the answer without using words or numbers. We are drawing on the creative side of your thinking, which provides a different perspective and insight to the usual verbal articulation of your purpose.

It is important that you keep the question in mind and don't put any limitations in place. Limitations like family commitments and financial commitments are real for most leaders, but for this exercise I would like you to assume there are no limiting factors. Once you have completed this exercise, you should have tapped into different perspectives on what you would like your life to be like if there were no limits or restrictions in place. Now take a moment to think how you might verbally articulate your drawing to someone else that might be able to help you achieve this life in the future.

This drawing exercise often brings clarity to a leader's purpose in life. Amazingly, most leaders tell me that they have never shared this clear vision with anyone else. They haven't previously had the clarity or courage to share their dream with others to help them achieve the life they want. The drawing is only part of the exercise. More importantly, you need to share your articulation of this drawing with close friends, associates and your boss. By sharing your vision with as many people as possible, you will start to feel a momentum and inner drive to help bring it to reality.

When you share the vision, do so with only curiosity in mind. Don't be judgmental about the reaction you receive from those around you. Simply share the vision and then ask them the question, 'If you were in my shoes right now, what would you do next to achieve the life I have described?' This process often highlights incorrect assumptions about limiting factors such as money and family commitments. If others understand how you want to live your life, they are usually happy to support you in amazing ways.

Finally, this process is most successful when you ask others around you to hold you to account regarding the next steps you have decided to take. This can be informal accountability or more formal feedback sessions. We all need help and support in achieving our dreams. Make sure you ask for it.

Chapter summary

- Leaders can easily lose their way in life if they don't understand their purpose.

- 50% of leaders are not totally clear about their purpose in life.

- We can become disconnected from the values and purpose that exist within the organisations we work for.

- We can become addicted to becoming successful in life without really understanding why we are doing what we are doing.

- Having purpose enables us to feel fulfilled in life and to focus on short- and long-term goals.

- Understanding the energisers and drains in your life can help you rediscover your purpose.

- Understanding who you are in service of can help you rediscover your purpose.

- Thinking about the legacy you want to leave behind can help you Reconnect with your purpose.

- Being creative when thinking about your purpose can provide you with more clarity about what you want in your future.

Actions

- Complete the energisers and drains exercise.

- Complete the 'in service of' exercise.

- Complete the legacy exercise.

- Complete the creative drawing exercise.

- Articulate your drawing into a compelling vision about your future by writing down six sentences that summarise the drawing. Make a list of the short- and long-term goals that will enable you to live this life.

- Tell ten people in your life about your vision and ask for their help in achieving it. Ask them what they would do in your shoes to move closer to the vision.

- Use the insight gained from the exercises above to design an ideal role description and charter. This will have all the energisers, and a one-page charter on what you will say yes and no to in terms of the next role in your life to enable you to keep your focus when exploring potential opportunities as and when they arise.

- If you are currently in a role, if it is appropriate, tell your organisation what your vision is and ask for help in achieving it. What roles within the organisation might be a good fit? What do you need to do to achieve a move into this kind of role?

- If the ideal role does not exist in your current organisation, build a succession plan in your company and clearly communicate your plan to exit over time. Tell the external market about your vision.

Amy's actions

Action notes from coaching session
Why am I here?
Top Energisers are leading people, making a difference in the world, being around family and friends, learning every day and being in charge of my own destiny. I need to make sure that I can access all of these as I develop in the COO role.
I am in service of my family, the Board of Fortune Industries, Carlos, my team, myself and the disadvantaged people around the world that benefit from our products. To date I have only focused on Carlos, my team and my family.
The legacy exercise taught me that I want to be remembered like my mother was. I want to make a difference in the world and stay close to my family.

Action notes from coaching session

6 sentences that describe my drawing:

I want to be there for my family when they need me.

I want to be there for my team when they need me.

I want to be the best version of myself every day of my life.

I want to make a difference in the world by helping disadvantaged families to have better lives.

I want to learn something new every day.

In five years' time I want to have choices about what I do with the rest of my life.

I have committed to share this vision with my family and friends and Carlos so that they can help me achieve it in the next five years.

4
Emotional Intelligence

Amy was enjoying her coaching sessions. Her coach was satisfied that she had reconnected with who she was and what was important to her, and felt that she could now work towards being the authentic version of herself. It had always existed, but wasn't always present in her key relationships. Amy was curious about the concept of emotional intelligence and understood that the next few months were going to be tough, but rewarding. She was hoping to become more aware of how her actions affected her own thoughts and the feelings of others around her.

She decided to confide in her team that she was going to be working hard on being the best version of herself each day. She openly expressed her concerns about how some of her bad habits might get in the way, and established a simple process for her team members to give her feedback the moment they observed those behaviours.

Over the last twenty years there have been many research studies that support the hypothesis that leaders with high emotional intelligence outperform leaders with high IQ. The Oxford English Dictionary defines emotional intelligence as 'the capacity to be aware of, control, and express one's emotions and to handle interpersonal relationships judiciously and empathetically'[14]. It is critical to focus on building and maintaining your emotional intelligence throughout your career to enable you to achieve your short- and long-term goals.

Why many leaders struggle to develop their emotional intelligence

Developing a healthy balance of IQ and emotional intelligence (EQ) can support leaders with building their self-leadership skills and managing their relationships with others. It is an effective leadership style that leads to higher performance levels over time, but many leaders choose not to develop their emotional intelligence. Instead, they decide to use their highly-attuned IQ and work as hard as they can each day to cope with whatever is thrown at them. They role-model leadership they have seen in the past. These are some of the issues that can get in the way of them making the right decisions:

---

14 'Emotional intelligence', www.lexico.com/definition/emotional_intelligence

- The leader has been promoted on the basis of having a strong technical or functional background and builds credibility through what they know and the authority they have as the leader.

- Many leaders have high IQ and rely on this to enable them to make effective decisions in complex situations. As they become more senior, they believe that focusing on their IQ to make effective decisions becomes more important, and they forget about the importance of building trust and strong relationships across the business.

- Many leaders are encouraged to become more effective by learning from supposed role models in their organisations and by attending leadership development programmes that teach them how to become better leaders. They learn from the 'outside in' rather than from the 'inside out'.

- Many leaders are often not held accountable by their boss or their board, so there is a tendency to try and hold themselves to account. They take on the habits and schedules of predecessors and fit in around others.

Many leaders choose to spend their time managing situations and people rather than leading from positions of high emotional intelligence. In the global leadership survey undertaken by the Tallents Partnership, 85% of respondents stated that they were extremely aware of how they impacted others with their behaviour and actions.[15] This was one of the most surprising results of the global leadership survey because many leaders act inconsistently around others. The result may be a reflection that leaders are generally not as aware as they think they are. When I ask clients to rate their awareness on a scale of 1 to 10, many of them rate themselves above 7, but their rating using an emotional intelligence analysis tool is usually much lower.

The benefits of building emotional intelligence

Research has shown that when leaders start to build their emotional intelligence, their overall performance improves significantly over time. They start to create time and space to think about how they are feeling about themselves in relationships, and how they go about completing tasks.

They learn how to become more present in relationships and in key moments in their day-to-day leadership responsibilities. This leads to becoming more engaged as leaders and more aware of their impact on others in the moment. They reflect on how they impact others, and ask for feedback on how they can behave differently to be more effective in their roles.

---

15   Tallents Partnership Leadership Survey (April 2021)

They also learn to control their emotions. This allows them to make decisions based on facts and gut instinct rather than irrational feelings that have been created by a lack of self-confidence and/or fear of failure. Their improved self-awareness allows them to be more agile in the moment and react to challenging situations effectively.

Building emotional intelligence allows leaders to hold themselves accountable more easily. They are able to think clearly about how their feelings affect their ability to deliver against their purpose and their long-term goals and react accordingly. Over time, these leaders develop their own authentic leadership style.

Four key areas of emotional intelligence

In his book *Emotional Intelligence: Why it can matter more than IQ,* psychologist Daniel Goleman identifies four key areas of emotional intelligence that we all have access to as human beings.[16] These are especially important to leaders striving to self-coach and improve their emotional intelligence. Consider which of the areas you may need to personally focus on:

1. **Self-awareness** is the ability to read and manage your own emotions.

---

16   D Goleman, *Emotional Intelligence: Why it can matter more than IQ* (Bloomsbury Publishing, 1995)

2. **Self-management** is the ability to keep your emotions in balance, adapt to your environment and focus on achieving your goals while maintaining a positive outlook on life.

3. **Social awareness** is the ability to show empathy toward others and to understand group and organisation dynamics.

4. **Relationship management** is the ability to influence and lead others while managing conflict effectively, and coaching and mentoring team members.

Leadership styles

In March 2000, Daniel Goleman was involved in a research study that was published in the Harvard Business Review.[17] He outlined six main leadership styles that have emerged from the emotional intelligence competencies:

1. **Coercive:** This leadership style demands immediate compliance. The key message is, 'Do what I tell you!' This style tends to work best in a crisis, in turnaround situations, or when dealing with challenging employees.

---

17 D Goleman, 'Leadership that gets results' (Harvard Business Review, April 2006), https://hbr.org/2000/03/leadership-that-gets-results, accessed 23 September 2021

2. **Authoritative:** This leadership style mobilises people towards a vision. The key message is, 'Come with me.' This style tends to work best when change management programmes are required or a new direction needs to be decided quickly.

3. **Affiliative:** This leadership style creates harmony and builds long-term bonds. The key message is, 'People come first.' This style tends to work best when there is negative conflict within the team or where employees need motivating in stressful situations.

4. **Democratic:** This leadership style forges consensus through participation. The key message here is, 'What do you think?' This style tends to work best when there is a need to gain buy-in or to get valuable input from key employees.

5. **Pacesetting:** This leadership style sets high standards for performance. The key message here is, 'Do as I do, now!' This style tends to work best when results are needed in the short term from a highly performing team.

6. **Coaching:** This leadership style develops people for the future. The key message here is, 'Try this.' This style tends to work best when long-term human capital development is crucial for sustainable success.

Goleman's research suggests that highly emotion-ally intelligent leaders will flex their leadership style depending on the situation they find themselves in. Two out of the six leadership styles highlighted are more likely to have a negative impact on organisa-tional culture and long-term performance: the coercive and the pacesetting styles. It's interesting to note the key messages in these leadership styles: 'Do what I tell you!' and 'Do as I do, now!' This confirms that the old, dominating leadership styles are no longer fit for purpose and that the other four leadership styles will be more effective in the future.

Measuring emotional intelligence

Before we make any decision, we have a thought. This thought leads to an emotion, and this emotion influ-ences our decision-making. If we can become more self-aware of our thoughts and the emotions they evoke, we can start to manage our emotions more effectively.

There are several emotional intelligence measurement tools in the marketplace. The one I use most is The Discovery Process® tool.[18] This tool enables a leader to complete a survey about how they manage their emo-tions and provides an output measure across the three different thinking styles assessed by The Discovery Process®. The three thinking styles plus six dimensions

18   CCR3™ Performance Management Discovery Process®, CCR3.com

of thought are split across the way we think about the external world and the way we think about ourselves. The profile measures 'how a person thinks and makes decisions' as a leader. It's not necessarily about 'managing their emotions' but their 'ability to manage their emotions' that's far more important. That's a big difference between the behavioural emotional intelligence and the actual emotional intelligence that this particular profile measures.

External clarity

Our external clarity demonstrates our potential to reach peak performance in our decision-making. The three dimensions of thought in relation to external clarity are:

- People

- Problem-solving

- Big-picture thinking

Imagine that you and I are in a room together having a chat. Without warning, the chair I am sitting on breaks and I fall onto the floor. If your dominant way of thinking about making sense of the external world is focused on people, then your immediate thought will be, 'Is Andrew OK?' Your next action will probably be to help me back to my chair.

If your dominant way of making sense of the external world is focused on problem-solving, then your immediate thought will be, 'How do I fix the chair?' Your next action will probably be to assess the chair to see if you can fix it.

If your dominant way of making sense of the external world is focused on the big picture, then your immediate thought will be, 'How do I put the system back in place?' Your next action will probably be replacing the broken chair with another one, asking me to sit on it, and then continuing the discussion where we left off.

If we have high levels of emotional intelligence, we can change our dominant thinking styles at any moment, but if our emotional intelligence is low, then our habitual way of thinking will automatically appear. The next time you have a meeting online or face-to-face, notice how people are thinking by what they choose to talk about. Is it people, problems or the big picture? By practising all three thinking styles each day we can train our brains to use the most effective style in the moment and improve our emotional intelligence.

Internal clarity

The three dimensions of thought in relation to internal clarity are:

- High self-esteem

- Our roles and purpose in life

- The direction we are heading

Imagine that your external clarity of thinking is the high-performance engine of a sports car and you are sitting in the driver's seat. You're about to press your foot down on the accelerator knowing that there is a tight corner a mile ahead.

For you to fulfil your potential as a human being, you need to have the confidence in your own ability and trust your experience and skill to take the corner at the correct speed and remain safe. This is where the three dimensions of internal clarity of thought come in. For us to be able to reach our full potential we need to have *high self-esteem*, be clear about our *roles and purpose in life* and be clear about the *direction we are heading* in our career and personal life. If we have clarity in these three areas then we feel good about ourselves and ready to fulfil our potential in making sense of the external world.

Many leaders have quite high external clarity of thought, but lower internal clarity, so much of the coaching and self-coaching is focused on how they view themselves and their ability to fulfil their potential. The journey to developing your emotional intelligence is a long and challenging adventure. There will be times when you feel you are making breakthroughs and times you fall back to old habits. This is normal for all of us. It takes time to develop our emotional intelligence. It is important to reflect frequently on how you are leading yourself and others in the management of feelings and relationships using the insight gained from this chapter.

Chapter summary

- Emotional intelligence is the ability to manage how we feel about ourselves and our relationships effectively over time.

- Many leaders tend to rate their emotional intelligence levels more highly than they are in reality.

- Many leaders tend to focus on using their IQ and experience to lead their organisations rather than develop their emotional intelligence.

- Leaders who build their emotional intelligence improve their personal and organisational performance over time.

- The four key components of emotional intelligence are self-awareness, self-management, social awareness and social skill.

- There are six main leadership styles that are built on emotional intelligence competencies, two of which are not helpful to long-term business performance.

- Our own emotional intelligence can be measured by assessing the six dimensions of thought: people, problem-solving, big-picture thinking, self-esteem, role and purpose, and direction in life.

- It is important to take time out to reflect on how we are developing our emotional intelligence and ask for support and feedback in how we manage our own emotions in relation to others.

Actions

- Look at the four components of emotional intelligence. Assess which areas you are strong in and which areas you are weaker in. Give yourself a score out of 10 for each area. Share your thoughts with another leader you respect and compare notes.

- Think about the six dimensions of thought used to measure emotional intelligence and give yourself a score out of 10 for each dimension. Think about one thing you can do tomorrow to start to raise one of your scores.

- To help move forward on this journey, think about the next couple of weeks in your life.

- Look at where you can create some time and space to think before you act on an important decision or before an important meeting. Become more aware of how you are feeling and whether you need to start thinking in a different way to create different feelings.

- Become more present in the moment more often so that you can become more aware of how you are impacting others when they are in your presence.

- Take time out to reflect on the type of leadership styles highlighted in this chapter that you may have modelled recently. Was it a conscious decision or habit?

Amy's actions

Action notes from coaching session
Emotional intelligence
4 components of EI
Self-awareness - 7 out of 10
Self-management - 5 out of 10
Social awareness - 7 out of 10
Social skills - 7 out of 10
6 dimensions of thought
People 6
Problem-solving 8
Big-picture thinking 4
Self-esteem 6
Role & purpose 7
Direction in life 7

Which leadership styles did I use today?

It was interesting to think about this. During the day I used the pacesetting style without thinking about it as I just needed to get some things across the line. But I also used the coaching style with my team when discussing a long-term project. I need to take more time out to reflect on the styles I am using each day and become more intentional in the use of the styles.

My coach has asked me to complete the EI discovery process so that I can gain more insight into where my strengths and weaknesses are in relation to my EI.

PART TWO
REFOCUS

5

What Is Essential?

Amy had been in her role for four months and was feeling more authentic in her leadership style. She felt that she better understood who she was, why she was here, and that there was a clear path in how she could fulfil her own purpose in life and still deliver on her company objectives. She had been working on becoming more aware of how her feelings and actions impacted her own behaviour and those of her colleagues. In her next coaching session, it emerged that even though the path was clear, Amy was becoming more aware that she couldn't attend to all the problems she came across as she walked along that path.

Her coach encouraged her to focus on only doing what was essential in her job to maximise her chances of success. Amy had not thought about this concept before. She learned that there were only a few essential things that only she could do. She set about changing the way she managed her work and knew deep down that she would

need to improve her delegation skills in the coming months.
She also knew that creating new habits was going to be
tough, so once again, she shared her thinking with her team
and asked for their help in holding her to account when she
was distracted from her essential tasks list.

It is critical to focus on what is essential for you to do in any stage of your career to achieve your short- and long-term goals, but many leaders choose not to. The Tallents Partnership global leadership survey found that only 2% of respondents stated that they spent all of their time on essential tasks that only they could do.[19]

Why leaders don't focus on what is essential

Many leaders can be task-oriented and tend to be reactive to requests on their time. They don't spend time planning to be proactive. Leaders invariably decide what goes in their diary, but tend to have too many meetings scheduled and don't build in time for reflection. When a leader starts in a new role, they inherit a job description and budgets and goals that were relevant before they arrived in the role. They fall into the same work patterns and habits as the previous incumbent. When leaders are finding their feet in a new role they don't tend to challenge or question what is expected of them as they navigate their way around the new organisation.

---

19   Tallents Partnership Leadership Survey (April 2021)

Many leaders are subservient to their bosses or boards and take instructions and guidance from them on how the role should be performed without challenging the outcomes and goals required of the role. For many leaders it is far easier to say yes to requests than to politely refuse and explain why it is not appropriate for them to undertake certain tasks. How many times have you agreed to take something on knowing that you don't have the time to do the best job possible? It is always easier to say yes to bosses, boards and key stakeholders.

Many leaders are also poor at delegating non-essential tasks to their team members or peers because they like to maintain control. It is sometimes perceived to be easier to do it themselves than to delegate and then have to redo it when the team member doesn't do it as anticipated.

Focusing on what is essential

When leaders do work towards focusing on what is essential:

- They do fewer tasks and start to create time and space to think about essential relationships and strategy.

- They take delight in saying no to a request when it is not essential to their role. This becomes easier over time, particularly when they identify other people that can help the person that has made the request.

• As they remove non-essential tasks, they begin to delegate more effectively. Team members start to become more engaged as they expand their roles to support their leader. This encourages the team members to identify what is essential to them, and in turn, they remove non-essential tasks from their daily schedules.

• The leader can hold themselves accountable more easily as they have fewer tasks and relationships to focus on. As they explain to others what their essential duties are, they ask for support from peers and team members to help hold them to account and stop them meddling in non-essential tasks.

Essentialism

Although many of the ideas in Greg McKeown's book *Essentialism: The disciplined pursuit of less* are not new, he does explain and convey the importance of disciplined focus on the 'pursuit of less' as being critical to leadership success in the world we live in today. One of his opening statements struck a chord with me when I read the book for the first time: 'Prioritise your life before somebody else does it for you.'[20]

---

20   G McKeown, *Essentialism: The disciplined pursuit of less* (Virgin Books, 2014)

As the leader of your own life, only you can know the priorities that are important to you. Every job description can be interpreted in a variety of ways and it is important to define who you want to be in the role. It is important for you to explore and evaluate what is truly important to you in life rather than allowing others to dictate what they think is important for you. Once you know what is truly important, you can start to remove tasks and relationships that don't add value to what is important to you. You can focus on executing only the essential tasks, removing any obstacles that stop you focusing on what is important to you. This philosophy is simple, but difficult to execute if you are not disciplined in your 'pursuit of less'.

To support you on this journey, it is important to understand that an essentialist thinks almost everything we do is not essential to leading a successful and fulfilling life. We have the power to choose how we spend our time and where we expend our energy to lead fulfilling lives. If you take a few moments to think about leaders that you know and your own workload, it is likely that almost everything that surrounds you is noise and that few relationships and tasks are really valuable. Contrary to many organisational change programmes, essentialism argues that making something better means subtracting something. Too many change programme leaders choose to focus on complexity and wonder why others are not prepared to follow.

How to become an essentialist

To become an essentialist, you need to go through the steps discussed in previous chapters. Then ask yourself the question: 'What is essential for me to do to live a fulfilling life?' Another way to consider the question is by asking yourself: 'If I could only do one thing with my life right now that would allow me to lead a successful and fulfilling life, what would I do?' Take a few minutes to write down your thoughts.

Now consider another, more important, question in relation to your answer (or to your current role): 'What are the essential things I need to do to be successful in life and at work that I, and only I, can do?' Bear in mind that some things that might be essential for you to be successful don't always need to be done by you. You should be able to write a list of between five and ten things that are essential to living the life you want that you, and only you, can do. These are the things that you should spend most of your time doing.

Chapter summary

- The road to essentialism involves developing self-leadership and asking the questions, 'Who am I? Why am I here?'

- Only 2% of leaders spend all their time on essential tasks and relationships.

- Many leaders find it extremely hard to focus on what is essential due to the legacy of previous incumbents in their role.

- Leaders can improve their own performance by focusing on what is essential.

- One of the most important questions in life is, 'What is essential that I, and only I, can do to ensure I am successful?'

- Answering this will allow leaders to focus on what is essential and remove the non-essential.

- Leaders need to ask for support in moving towards essentialism and delegating more effectively.

- Leaders can use the extra time gained by delegation to focus more on what is essential.

Actions

- Revisit the two key questions in this chapter:

  - If you could only do one thing with your life right now that would enable you to lead a successful and fulfilling life, what would you do?

  - What are the things that are essential for you to do to be successful in life and at work that you, and only you, can do?

- Take some time to think deeply about these questions:

    - Use the creative skills you learned in the second chapter to try drawing the answers to these questions.

    - List a couple of sentences that answer the first question.

    - List up to eight essential tasks that only you can do.

- Write down all the things that you intend to do (or are expected to do) by others in the next couple of weeks.

- Make a note of how many of these things are essential for you to be successful in life and that only you can do.

- Make a list of all the things that you can remove and eliminate from the diary in the next two weeks, including all non-essential tasks and any essential tasks that you can delegate to others.

- Once you have completed this exercise, practise saying no to all non-essential tasks or those that can be delegated to others from now on. You'll feel better for it.

Amy's actions

Action notes from coaching session

Only focus on what is essential

Q1 To lead a fulfilling life it is essential for me to be in charge of my own destiny and to make the biggest difference in the world by leading the organisation I choose to work for.

Q2 Essential tasks that only I can do

Lead my team

Manage my relationship with Carlos

Manage my relationship with the Board

Look after my own wellbeing

Represent Fortune Industries on the global sustainable futures stage

Be present as a loving family member

Take time out to focus on reflection and strategy

6
Trust

Amy was sitting in her study and had an hour free before her next video call meeting. She reflected on her progress during the last month and was pleased with where she was spending her time. She noticed that she had become more disciplined in delegating non-essential tasks and that she scheduled more time with her key stakeholders. She actually felt good about politely saying no when asked to spend her time on non-essential tasks. Amy's key stakeholders were becoming much clearer about the important role she was playing in the organisation.

Her coach had asked her what her key stakeholders thought about her performance in the role so far, and in truth, she didn't know. Amy made too many assumptions about how much trust existed in her key stakeholder relationships. She committed to finding out how much they trusted her, and if it wasn't enough, she was going to be proactive in building trust. She knew she would need her stakeholders to support and trust her when her role became more challenging in the future. She was also struggling to manage her remote team as effectively as she would have liked when she delegated non-essential tasks. She knew there was a trust issue on her side. Her coach had encouraged her to be more courageous in her vulnerability about her lack of trust in the team. She knew that she needed to spend more time with each of them to get to know them better and make them aware of her difficulties in trusting others.

It is critical to focus on building trust with the key stakeholders who have the ability to influence your future success, but many leaders choose not to build trust with key stakeholders in their lives. Instead, they decide to wait for the stakeholder to build trust with them – particularly difficult stakeholders who are enigmas and play their cards close to their chests. It is easier to spend time elsewhere rather than investing in the key stakeholder relationships.

In the Tallents Partnership survey, 44% of respondents stated that they were not confident that their key stakeholders had full trust in their relationships with the leader.[21]

Why leaders find it difficult to build trust

Many leaders have a lack of understanding about who their key stakeholders are. Stakeholders can range

---

21 Tallents Partnership Leadership Survey (April 2021)

from shareholders to customers, and everything in between. Leaders often believe that they are in control of their own future and that they can determine how successful they will be without much support. The reality is that all leaders need key stakeholders to be supportive of them through thick and thin. There is an argument to suggest that most of a leader's time should be spent building relationships with key stakeholders so that they can rely on their support when it is most needed.

Leaders may find it difficult to rebuild trust with key stakeholders when they perceive they have been let down by others in the past. Many leaders don't want to show their vulnerability by making the first move in building trust. They are uncomfortable showing vulnerability as they believe this is a display of weakness, but being human and vulnerable is one of the key ways in which we build trust with others. Sometimes, pride and misplaced expectations that others should build trust with leaders first get in the way of strong relationships. When this doesn't happen, they wonder why relationships are not as strong as they should be.

Many leaders also make assumptions about how key stakeholders feel about them. They don't have enough trust in their relationships to ask them directly or know that the answer they receive is honest and delivered with the best intentions to support and build the relationship further. You can only get truly honest feedback from stakeholders when you trust each other.

Many leaders lack the self-awareness of how their lack of trustworthiness affects their decision-making and their impact on others' ability to make effective decisions. They can't determine the likely outcomes of decisions because they don't know the level of trust in their relationships. Many leaders suffer from imposter syndrome and have low levels of self-confidence in their ability to build trust with experienced and influential stakeholders. This leads to further self-doubt and avoidance of building trust. Key people around the leader start to lose confidence in them and may take on more responsibility for their own actions, which can lead to a silo mentality permeating within the organisation.

Leaders often choose to spend their time managing situations and people rather than leading from positions of trust in their key stakeholder relationships.

Building trust with key stakeholders

Once a leadership team understands what all of their key stakeholders need, it can lead to an opportunity to change the way the organisation is structured, or indeed, the way the whole system they are part of operates. For example, Uber understood that customers wanted more choice and flexibility in the way they moved around cities. Their needs were not being met by local government operating systems, and licensed taxi firms were expensive to operate. By understanding their customers better, Uber managed to change a whole industry by delivering what their customers really wanted.

If leaders really understand their key stakeholders' needs, it enables them to think more deeply about meaningful organisation and team goals that serve their various stakeholders. Involving stakeholders in goal-setting can be a liberating experience for leadership teams rather than the mundane annual budgeting and revenue target-setting goals we have all become used to.

Once goals are aligned with stakeholder needs, it becomes clearer how the organisation needs to be structured to meet those goals, and the organisation becomes more efficient. Many organisations structure themselves based on past performance and already achieved goals. Understanding stakeholders' needs means that we might be able to remove product ranges that are no longer relevant or serve customers through a different operating model.

Building strong relationships with key stakeholders enables the leader to hold themselves accountable more easily as they are able to think clearly about how key stakeholders will react to the decisions and actions they take to deliver against their purpose and their long-term goals. They can do this effectively because they have built trust within their relationships and are trusted to do the right thing by the organisation.

Edelman Trust Barometer

Over the last twenty years, Edelman, one of the world's largest communication firms, has produced an annual global research study called the Edelman Trust Barometer.[22] Each year, the company surveys over 34,000 people in twenty-eight countries and measures the public's trust in a variety of institutions and organisations. It is widely accepted as the definitive study regarding the trust we have in the organisations that serve the planet.

Over the last two decades, trust has been eroded to the extent that the public now have more trust in NGOs and businesses than they do in government bodies and marketing agencies. This has profound implications in how governments can regain the trust of their populations over the next decade, and it will involve stronger collaboration between private and public sector organisations. For anyone wanting to build trust with key stakeholders, these are a must-read.

---

22 www.edelman.co.uk/research, accessed 17 September 2021

Stakeholder mapping

This is a powerful tool that raises awareness around who your key stakeholders are, and what level of trust currently exists in the relationships. A practical example will bring this concept to life. Think of a CEO of a hospital trust at the start of the Covid pandemic. Their immediate thought, quite rightly, would have been, 'How do we structure ourselves to cope with the increase in seriously ill patients and to save as many lives as possible?' One possibility is to clear as many hospital beds as possible and ensure that the staff are as prepared as they can be for what is to come. A hospital CEO who has stakeholder relationships at the heart of their thinking would then take time to list the various stakeholders that would have an interest in how the hospital intended to manage the crisis.

Once they stated the goal of saving as many lives as possible, the CEO would need to not only understand the stakeholders' views on achieving this goal, but also what the stakeholders would need to be able to support the CEO in achieving this goal. The care-home sector stakeholder, for example, may not feel fully prepared to receive patients from hospitals. The CEO would need to recognise that they needed central and local government reassurance that PPE equipment would be readily available to cope with the influx of patients from hospitals. The union's concerns regarding their members' safety would also have to be considered to gain the support of the union for the CEO's strategy. By understanding each stake-holder and what their needs are, the CEO is more likely to be able to reach the goal of saving as many lives as possible.

How many CEOs invest the time in understanding their key stakeholders? How do we make sure that we spend our time with the right stakeholder, at the right time, to maximise the chances of being successful, meeting our goals and feeling fulfilled in what we do? Take five minutes to make a list of all the key stakeholders that you can think of that are either interested in your future success or happiness, and all the stakeholders that you currently, or will, serve in some way. Many of us have so many stakeholders and so little time.

A stakeholder map can relate to your own personal success or the success of your team or business. In any stakeholder map, you are at the centre of the map. You need to ask yourself the question: 'For me to be successful and fulfilled in the life I have chosen for myself, who has a stake in my future success and who do I serve as I live that life?'

The map below is Amy's stakeholder map. Amy is at the centre, and she has placed the various stakeholders she can think of on the map. Where they are placed on the map depends on the level of trust in their relationship. For example, Amy's family is placed close to her because there is a high level of trust within her family relationships. Her PA is someone she trusts, but she is

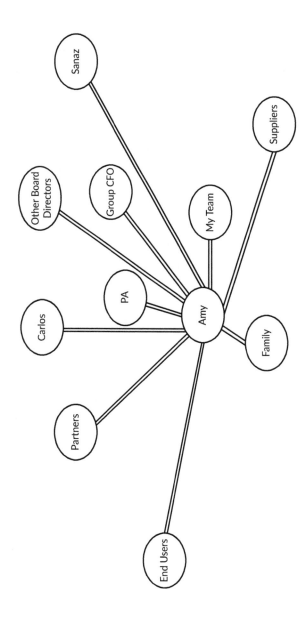

Amy's Stakeholder Map

not close to her family, so she needs to be placed close to Amy, but not near the family. She added Carlos to the map further away than her PA as she is still building trust with Carlos. Sanaz is a senior non-executive director with an operations background and has been interested in Amy's progress over recent months. Sanaz is the furthest away from Amy as she has no relationship with her yet. Using the same rules, Amy has added her partners and suppliers until she has mapped all her key stakeholders.

What this map shows is where Amy is in her relationship with each key stakeholder. The closer they are to Amy, the stronger the relationship and the better understanding they have of each other. They can rely on each other. The further away the stakeholder is, the weaker the relationship is and the less certain Amy is about their needs and how they might be able to support her.

This exercise increases our awareness of who has the ability to influence our personal success and wellbeing. Take some time to build your own stakeholder map for your own personal situation. Ask yourself the question: 'For me to be successful and fulfilled in the life I have chosen for myself, who has a stake in my future success and who else do I serve as I live that life?'

The next important step is to think about how important the stakeholders are in relation to your future success. On the diagram below, Amy has allocated a score between 1 and 10 against each stakeholder. 1 means that they are not important to her future

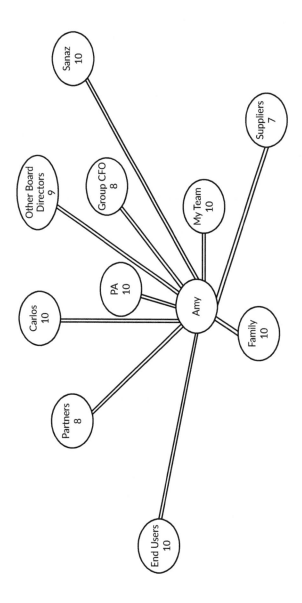

Amy's Stakeholder Map: Importance of Stakeholders

success and 10 means they are critical. What is interesting about this map is that Amy has some critical stakeholders quite far away from her on the map.

Take some time to allocate scores to your own stakeholders on your own map. Now your stakeholder map contains some key information for you. What are you going to do with it? Who are the key stakeholders where you believe the relationship is important enough for you to invest time in making the relationship stronger? Only you can initiate action to strengthen the relationship. You cannot expect the stakeholders to make the first move, as they have other priorities in their lives.

Project Aristotle

In 2012, Google embarked on a project that would fundamentally change the way they built their business going forward. They were curious to know what was behind high-performance teams. They studied 180 teams across Google's global organisation over a period of two years looking for clues about why the most successful teams performed so well. The findings surprised them. What became apparent was that psychological safety (another word for trust) was the key ingredient to high-performing teams. It is worth reading the more detailed papers and research that support their findings.[23]

---

23 Google 're:Work Guide: Understand team effectiveness', no date, https://rework.withgoogle.com/print/guides/5721312655835136, accessed 17 September 2021

The 'emotional trust bank'

In *The 7 Habits of Highly Effective People*, Covey talks about trust being 'the glue of life'[24] and describes the concept of the 'emotional trust bank'.[25] Let's use a simple example to bring his idea to life.

In your relationship with a friend or partner, there are times when you make trust deposits. You get home on time, you take the rubbish out each night, you remember anniversaries and birthdays. You keep your promises and go beyond your commitments out of love and gratitude. The trust balance in the trust bank looks healthy and your friend or partner will feel more inclined to support you in times of need.

At some point in the relationship, you become distracted by other thoughts and events and you start to come home later than agreed. You miss mealtimes and start to forget jobs you agreed to do around the house. Now the trust balance is low and it is much harder to ask the other person to trust you when they need you. This is a simple concept but it really does help us to assess where our key relationships are right now.

---

24 S Covey, A Roger Merrill and RR Merrill, *First Things First* (Prentice Hall & IBD, 1994)
25 S Covey, *The 7 Habits of Highly Effective People*

Lencioni's Trust Pyramid

Patrick Lencioni's book *The Five Dysfunctions of a Team: A leadership fable* centres around a business fable highlighting the five dysfunctions that stop teams becoming high-performing.[26] He highlights these dysfunctions in a Trust Pyramid. His premise is that teams must work upwards from the base of the pyramid through each layer to the top of the pyramid.

You cannot proceed to the second level until there is complete trust in the team. Once trust exists, there can be open conflict between team members that is focused on differences and how to work together to accommodate each other. Once conflict has been resolved properly, team members are more likely to be able to commit to each other in working towards the team goals. This then enables the team to create ways of holding each other accountable and will ultimately lead to better outcomes and business results.

The key here is that conflict resolution should only take place when team members feel safe to challenge each other, and this can only happen when they trust each other enough to challenge bad ideas and poor

---

26   P Lencioni, *The Five Dysfunctions of a Team: A leadership fable* (Wiley & Sons, 2002)

behaviours in service of the team goals. If you have not read this book, I encourage you to do so. It can lead to team performance improvements in a short period of time.

Nine Habits of Trust model

John Blakey, a former FTSE100 Divisional CEO, conducted in-depth research into what trust really is, and how we can measure it. When he asked CEOs the question, 'How important is trust to the success of your business?', the CEOs usually responded that it was absolutely critical. When he asked them how they measured how much trust existed in the organisation, the CEOs would refer him to the employee engagement survey that had been conducted twelve months ago. The truth was that the CEO didn't have a clue how much trust was in the organisation. John was keen to research the subject further and he published his book, *The Trusted Executive: Nine leadership habits that inspire results, relationships and reputation* in 2016.[27] In the book, John summarises his research findings and presents the three pillars that inspire trust, and his Nine Habits of Trust model.

---

27 J Blakey, *The Trusted Executive: Nine leadership habits that inspire results, relationships and reputation* (Kogan Page, 2016)

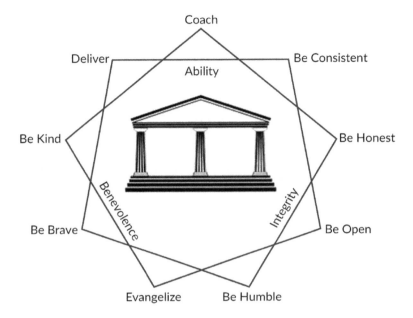

Coach

Deliver

Be Consistent

Ability

Be Kind

Be Honest

Benevolence

Integrity

Be Brave

Be Open

Evangelize   Be Humble

The Nine Habits of Trust Model[28]

As you can see from the diagram, Blakey identifies three pillars of trust that are needed to become trustworthy over time: ability, integrity and benevolence. The relationship between these three pillars is not linear. They are interdependent and you need to be strong in all three areas. We can all think of leaders who have ability and integrity but are ruthless and don't succeed in the long term. Likewise, we all know leaders who are kind and honest, but don't have the required ability to lead an organisation through tough times.

---

28   Adapted from J Blakey, *The Trusted Executive: Nine leadership habits that inspire results, relationships and reputation*

Blakey then outlines the nine habits that support these three pillars. If we develop and practise these key habits, we can build trust in our relationships.

For the ability pillar, the habits are: deliver, coach and be consistent. Do what you say you are going to do. Coach others to be the best they can be. Be consistent in your communication and your behaviour. These are all habits we can build and practise every day in our leadership roles.

For the integrity pillar the habits are: be honest, be open and be humble. This is where many leaders really struggle as they need to be vulnerable and authentic in their leadership style, and this is not always easy, particularly when the organisation culture discourages these habits.

For the benevolence pillar the habits are: evangelise, be brave and be kind. Again, these three habits can be tough to develop for leaders as they call for courage, self-confidence and trust in human nature.

All of these habits are difficult to develop in today's work environments, but certainly worth working towards. Think for a moment about the leader that you most admire and respect because of how you have experienced them. How many of the nine habits did they have?

Chapter summary

- Trust is the 'glue of life'.[29]

- 44% of leaders are not confident that their key stakeholders have complete trust in them as leaders.

- Many leaders find the reasons they have been successful to date can get in the way of building strong, trust-based relationships later in life.

- Building trust with key stakeholders is fundamental to personal and professional success in the long term.

- Stakeholder mapping is a critical first step in building trust in your key relationships.

- The 'trust bank' teaches us that to build trust, we must become trustworthy. We cannot make others trust us.

- Using the Lencioni and Blakey models, we can build trust with others and within our teams.

- We need to create time to review our relationships and spend time within them.

- We can work on building new habits of trust every day.

- We can ask for support and feedback in how we build trust with others and assess the strength of our relationships over time.

---

29 S Covey, A Roger Merrill and RR Merrill, *First Things First*

Actions

- Take a moment to think about a relationship that you are worried about. Think about the last few weeks and months. In terms of your actions, where is your trust balance now? What can you do to top up the trust balance and improve the relationship? Make a note of an action you can take to improve this relationship. (Doing an exercise like this emphasises that we cannot control what the other person in the relationship does. We can only invest in the relationship by building trust credits in the trust bank over time.)

- Think about your key stakeholder relationships. Build further on the map you have created for yourself. Identify at least one relationship that you need to focus on.

- Think about the nine habits. Score yourself out of 10 for each habit.

  - Which one can you work on in the coming weeks?

  - Which ones come naturally?

  - Who can you share your experiences with?

- Ask a close colleague or friend to rate you out of 10 against each habit and compare notes.

- Make at least one commitment to an action that works the habit and ask others to support you as you practise the habit.

Amy's actions

Action notes from coaching session
Trust
I am worried about the relationship with Sanaz. I don't know how much she trusts me. I am going to ask for a coffee meeting to get to know her better.
9 habits of trust model
Deliver 8
Coach 8
Be consistent 6
Be honest 6
Be open 6
Be humble 4
Evangelise 3
Be brave 5
Be kind 8

7
Accountability

Amy had been in her new role for six months. Her CEO, Carlos, was pleased with how she had been progressing and was seeing real improvements in how the business was being managed. Carlos was hands-off and did not need to spend a lot of time with Amy. In her next coaching session, she shared that even though things were going well, she was worried that she might not sustain her performance levels. As she became more comfortable in the role, she might take her foot off the pedal and coast for a while. Her coach encouraged her to think about who could help her retain her focus and hold her to account.

Amy knew what she had to do to keep true to her purpose and achieve her personal and professional goals. She spent time with her key stakeholders and explained where she needed to be held to account. She worked with each stakeholder to agree how they could best do that and agreed to gain regular feedback on how she was doing

*in regard to her commitments. She knew there would
be uncomfortable discussions ahead, and as she did not
like conflict situations, she agreed with her stakeholders
that any conflict would be resolved in a structured and
reflective space rather than in the heat of the moment.*

In any stage of your career, it is critical to focus on holding yourself and others to account to ensure that you maintain focus on what is important to deliver your future success. In the Tallents Partnership survey, 60% of respondents stated that they were not effective in holding themselves and others to account at work.

Why leaders find accountability difficult

When I coach clients about their role and their relationship with key stakeholders I ask the question, 'Who holds you to account?' There is usually a long pause while they think deeply about the question.

Think about this question yourself for a moment. Who is it that holds you to account in your relationships as you work towards your personal and career goals in your current role (or in a recent past role)?

Without exception, every single client I have ever worked with has answered, 'Me. I hold myself to account.' When I ask how their boss or board directors hold them to account, they tell me that they are set targets and have to explain any variances, but they don't feel truly held to account by anyone but themselves. This is a regular occurrence. It explains why so many organisations and leaders never achieve their full potential.

When new leaders are appointed into organisations, they are usually set targets and goals by their boss or their board and there is sometimes a lack of clarity in terms of what the goals really are. There are financial targets and shareholder returns to focus on, but the newly-appointed leader is usually left to define the strategic goals with their teams. They rarely seek to understand what their various stakeholders really expect from them. Leaders miss out on fantastic opportunities to partner with stakeholders in holding them and their teams to account.

Many leaders have a lack of understanding about how they can help others to hold themselves and their teams to account. They believe that they are in control of their own future and that they can determine how successful they will be without others holding them to account. The reality is that all leaders need key stakeholders to help hold themselves to account in delivering long-term goals. It is also almost impossible to hold others to account when it is clear that a leader can't consistently hold themselves to account.

Most of my clients make assumptions that their stakeholders are not interested in holding them to account, but what they are misunderstanding is how difficult it is for a variety of stakeholders to hold a leader to account when they are not in daily contact and don't understand the pressures that the leader is under. They have rarely tested these general assumptions. It is not common for leaders to ask stakeholders for help in being held accountable as they also fear that it won't be aligned with their own realistic goals. It is far easier to bury their heads in the sand and work towards goals without having their feet held to the fire by stakeholders.

The root cause of poor accountability management with many leaders tends to be their fear of conflict. It is easier to spend time elsewhere rather than investing time and energy in managing conflict effectively and building accountability within the organisation.

These factors all contribute towards leaders often choosing to spend their time managing situations and people rather than leading from positions of true accountability within an organisation.

Building accountability in your organisation

Building accountability in your organisation inevitably leads to improved organisational performance. Once the members of a leadership team understand how to hold one another to account, it can lead to an opportunity to focus on the key goals of the organisation in a more efficient way. A positive commercial tension is created in the team and everyone is more likely to be moving in the same direction.

Being vulnerable demonstrates how key stakeholders can help hold you to account. When things get tough or creative solutions are needed, you can rely on your stakeholders to help you focus to be successful in the long term.

Leaders that really understand how to hold themselves and others to account recognise triggers within themselves and their environments that steer them away from their personal and team goals. Involving stakeholders in managing the various triggers can be a liberating experience for leadership teams as it enables them to unlock higher performance levels over the long term.

Once the various internal and external triggers are understood, it becomes clearer how the organisation needs to be structured to meet their goals and the organisation becomes more efficient. Many organisations structure themselves based on past performance and already achieved goals. Understanding triggers that affect our performance means that we learn how we might be able to change our work environments or serve customers through a different operating model.

Building stronger relationships with key stakeholders enables the leader to hold themselves accountable more easily as they are able to think clearly about how key stakeholders will react to the decisions and actions they take to deliver against their purpose and their long-term goals. They can do this effectively because they have built trust within their relationships and are trusted to do the right thing by the organisation.

Managing triggers

In Marshall Goldsmith's book *Triggers: Sparking positive change and making it last,* he explores the reasons that leaders don't keep their promises.[30] 'Triggers' are events that lead to changes in our thoughts, feelings or behaviour. Human beings find it difficult to change their behaviour as we are creatures of habit, but we need to change our behaviours to keep our commitments and hold ourselves accountable.

There are two types of triggers that stop us keeping to our commitments. The first type are environmental triggers. These are triggers that are part of our day-to-day environment. They may be associated with organisational culture or market conditions or the way others behave. We cannot control these triggers, but we can decide how to react to them over time.

---

30   M Goldsmith, *Triggers: Sparking positive change and making it last* (Profile Books, 2016)

The second type of triggers are personal belief triggers. Examples include a leader that has a lack of self-confidence in their ability to deal with certain situations. It may be that they feel inferior to others who are better educated than them. It may be that they feel they are not good at presenting themselves to large groups of staff. These triggers stop us fulfilling our commitments to ourselves and others, but we can gain control of them and can manage them effectively over time.

If we can learn to manage our triggers in such a way that they don't steer us away from our commitments to ourselves and others, we are more likely to achieve our goals. Goldsmith suggests managing our triggers with the acronym AIWATT. It stands for 'Am I Willing At This Time to make the investment required to make a positive difference to this topic'. This is a simple question to ask yourself before acting after being triggered. The concept creates a delaying mechanism between the trigger and the behaviour that follows. It gives us time to consider a more positive response than the one we might normally choose.

'Am I willing?' implies that we are taking responsibility. Do I really want to do this? 'At this time' reminds us that we are operating in the present. Differing circumstances will demand a different response. The only issue is what we are facing right now.

As an example, let's assume that somebody at work makes a sarcastic comment about what you have just said in a meeting. This might normally trigger a response within you that you can't be bothered to deal with their pettiness at this time. You withdraw from the meeting and miss the opportunity to make a further, important point that would move the team closer to their goal.

By using AIWATT, you can decide whether you are willing to take responsibility right now to respond in a different way. You can ignore the sarcastic comment to make the positive contribution that the organisation deserves. You need to take time to consider your response rather than let your habitual behaviour control it. It may be that once you have considered AIWATT you still choose to behave in the same way, but at least it is a conscious decision.

Although AIWATT gives us a way to cope with both environmental and belief triggers in a reactive way, if we are going to make positive change with regard to accountability, we need to be more proactive in managing ourselves more effectively. Goldsmith's Six Daily Questions provides us with a process to support us in building proactive accountability habits.

Six Daily Questions

I encourage leaders to ask themselves six engaging questions at the end of each day and record their responses to them so they can be tracked. I also encourage them to relay their scores to a key stakeholder who has agreed to help hold them to account. Dropping someone an email or calling them at the end of the day or week to relay scores helps to keep leaders accountable. Although the leader can add as many engaging questions as they like that relate to their goals, Goldsmith's six questions, as listed here, are the ones that provide the most focus:

1. Did I do my best to set clear goals today?

2. Did I do my best to make progress towards my goals today?

3. Did I do my best to find meaning today?

4. Did I do my best to be happy today?

5. Did I do my best to build positive relationships today?

6. Did I do my best to be fully engaged today?

Using the questions above (or your own version of questions that are important to you), take a few minutes to give yourself a score for each question out of 10 relating to your behaviour yesterday. A score of 10 means 'I did my absolute best' and a score of 1 means 'I didn't try at all that day'. There are no right and wrong answers, this exercise helps you to gain insight into how you are holding yourself to account over time.

Now think about someone you could share your scores with today and consider letting them know how you want your score to move in the coming week. By regularly sharing how you are trying to keep your commitments, you are changing your habits over time and more likely to become more accountable for your actions.

Reflecting on your thoughts

In her book *Self-Coaching 101*, Brooke Castillo shares further ideas about how we can use our increasing emotional intelligence to manage our personal self-limiting beliefs more effectively.[31] We all find ourselves in certain circumstances that immediately trigger thoughts in our head. These cause certain feelings that then lead to certain actions and results. The premise of the book is that by taking time to reflect on our thoughts in relation to the circumstances we find ourselves in, we can change the results of our actions.

As an example, let's say that a key business partner of mine leaves me a voice message to give them a call back straight away. Due to my past relationship with the business partner, I believe that they are a bit self-important and that they believe that I should respond in the timeframe they have set.

---

31   B Castillo, *Self-Coaching 101* (Futures Unlimited Coaching, 2008)

The *circumstances* here are that my business partner has left me a message asking them to call back straight away. My *thoughts* are that they are just trying to show how important they are; that they are being unrealistic in expecting me to ring back straight away – I am as important and have many things to do. This leads to negative *feelings* of frustration, defensiveness, insecurity, defiance and being judgmental. This causes me to take no *action*. I don't ring them back straight away and choose to spend my time doing something more important. Ultimately, I don't ring them back until two days later. On this occasion, the *result* is negative. My business partner had wanted to share a lead for a piece of business that needed collaboration the next day.

In this example, the only thing that is factual is the message that was left. I made up the rest of the narrative with my thoughts. By reflecting on my thoughts and having the courage to change them, I may have ended up with a different result. A useful coping strategy is for us to come up with as many alternative thoughts as possible and see where they lead us.

In this example, my initial thought to the voice message could have been one of curiosity, which could have caused feelings of excitement and anticipation, which could have led to me responding quickly and finding out that my partner had a lead to share with me. I could have thought, 'I wonder how important it is to get back to them quickly?' This could have led to me feeling collaborative and fair, and this could have led to me sending them an email to ask how urgent it was and when was the latest I could ring them back? This would have prompted them to provide me with more information and I would have seen the importance of replying sooner rather than later.

These ideas provide us with another way of dealing with everyday triggers that come from our own thoughts. Take five minutes to think of a situation recently where you felt really negative about the circumstances you found yourself in:

- Write a few sentences about the *circumstances*.

- Write down what *thoughts* this created in your head.

- Write down what *feelings* this created within you.

- Write down what *actions* this led to.

- Finally, write down the *result* of your actions.

Once you have done this, do the same exercise with the same circumstances, but insert some other thoughts you could have had at the time and see what feelings and actions this could have led to. Try several different thoughts and notice how different the results might have been.

The journey to building accountability within your own organisation is a long and challenging adventure.

There will be times when you feel you are making breakthroughs and days when you are back to old habits. This is normal for all of us. It takes time to develop accountability, but it starts with us. Once we start role-modelling the right behaviours, we can support others who want to hold themselves accountable. Over time, each team member can learn how to support each other and team accountability will improve.

Chapter summary

- 60% of leaders are not effective at holding themselves and others to account at work.

- Successful leaders find it difficult to ask others to hold them to account.

- It is not easy to hold yourself to account, so ask for help.

- Building personal accountability over time supports high performance.

- Managing environmental and personal belief triggers more effectively can help build accountability over time.

- Practising AIWATT can help create a better response when we are triggered.

- Creating six engaging daily questions and asking for help in holding us to account builds useful daily habits.

- Using our emotional intelligence to change our thoughts in response to circumstances can lead to a change in results.

Actions

- Look for opportunities where you can create some thinking time in the next couple of weeks.

- Practise AIWATT the next time you become self-aware that you have been triggered.

- Create a list of six engaging questions to ask yourself each day and ask for help in holding you to account in living these habits.

- Think about a recent event where the circumstances led to negative thoughts and a negative outcome. Think about the different thoughts that you could have had to arrive at a different more positive outcome.

- Think about your key stakeholder relationships. Who can help to hold you to account?

- Ask others to support you as you practise holding yourself to account.

Amy's actions

Action notes from coaching session

Accountability

6 daily questions to ask myself:

Did I do my best to be available for my team today?

Did I do my best to manage my energy levels today?

Did I do my best to be kind to myself and others today?

Did I do my best to be happy today?

Did I do my best in building trust today?

Did I do my best in delegating tasks today?

8
Creating Space

Amy could see her efforts were paying off. Her relationships with her key stakeholders were stronger than ever. She was being held accountable around her commitments to focus on her essential tasks and delegating effectively. The weight of responsibility accompanying her newly-found accountability had forced Amy to focus on the short term during the first six months in the role. The market was becoming tougher, and technology was enabling competitors to challenge existing business models.

Carlos was a strong leader, but he enjoyed the customer-facing aspects of his role too much and Amy felt that not enough time was spent thinking about the future. Amy's coach encouraged her to think about how she could manage her time more effectively so that she could create more time to think.

In any stage of your career, it is critical to create space to think deeply about your relationships with yourselves and others. Time to think about how we are feeling and how we are progressing in our lives. Time to think about stakeholders and what they need from us. The global leadership survey undertaken by the Tallents Partnership showed that only 20% of respondents stated that they created enough time to think about the future of their organisation and their relationships with key people in their lives.

Why leaders struggle to create space in their lives

Many leaders choose not to create space and time in their daily lives as it sometimes needs intensive inner work that focuses on emotional events from the past and present. When I ask new clients about the things that hold them back in their current or most recent role, most explain that they don't have enough time to get everything done. I try to get them to understand that they have *chosen* not to have enough time to get things done. It doesn't just happen to them.

Most leaders make incorrect assumptions about what is important when they decide how to spend their time day-to-day. Post-Covid, there is immense pressure to be visible and on call on Zoom meetings all day to ensure they stay connected. Many leaders choose to do rather than think, but surely thinking is what the leader is getting paid for? They have a team of people that get things done. The team is often looking for clear direction from the leader, and this clarity can only be created by ensuring there is enough space to think.

Many leaders rarely ask stakeholders for help in creating space for them to think as they fear that it will be misunderstood as a display of weakness. It is far easier to bury their heads in the sand and work towards goals without having to say no to people to create the space that is needed. Leaders often choose to spend their time managing tasks and people and avoiding spending time on their own where they could work out how to lead from a position of courageous and considered leadership.

Benefits of creating space

Once a leader understands how to create space for themselves, it can lead to opportunities for further personal development. For example, a leader who takes time out to reflect on how effective a meeting was can think about ways to improve the overall team performance in future meetings.

Being vulnerable demonstrates how key stakeholders can help leaders to create precious space and time to think about key decisions that need to be made. When things get tough or creative solutions are needed, they can rely on their stakeholders to help them focus on what is really needed to be successful in the long term.

If leaders really understand how to create space for themselves, it enables them to think more deeply about a variety of situations that could challenge them, take them out of their comfort zone and build their self-confidence further. By creating more space, leaders often build their self-confidence and vulnerability, and this in turn enables them to become more decisive and courageous as a leader. Once leaders begin to create space for themselves, it also sets the tone for the rest of the organisations and inspires other employees to become more aware of how they can do the same.

How to create more space in your life

To create more space in your life, be aware of where you are spending your time and show that you are willing to change your habits with the support of others around you. Take a few minutes to look at your diary for the next two weeks and think about which meetings you really need to attend and see how much space you can create to think rather than meet. Work out where you could delegate the meeting organiser/ chair role to another team member. Which meetings could you stop attending? Which meetings could you attend for only part of the meeting?

Once you have completed this, work out how many hours you think you can create for thinking rather than doing. Block out time in your diary for space to think about important decisions and reflect on what has happened during the previous week. Look at your list of essential tasks that focuses on the things that you, and only you, can do to be successful in your role.

This exercise usually releases a few hours a week for leaders to start new habits in creating space and time to think.

What to do with the extra space and time you create

Firstly, a leader needs to create space and time to think. About anything. The first thing that comes into your head. How does it make you feel? What do you need to do? Who with? What can you reflect on from the previous day or earlier that day? The more deeply a leader can think about what needs to happen next, the more effective the decision is likely to be.

Secondly, a leader needs to create space to connect with key stakeholders. This is about being attentive and showing that you really care about how the key stakeholder feels. It means staying longer in a meeting because the stakeholder needs to be truly heard. The leader needs to have all the time in the world for their key stakeholders, yet many of these meetings tend to be cut short as the leader needs to go to the next meeting.

Next, a leader needs to create the space to *do*. This is about doing the limited essential things that the leader chooses to do to the best of their ability rather than at the last minute or flying by the seat of their pants. Being present in the activity and inspiring confidence in others is key when executing their key essential tasks.

Finally, and most importantly, a leader needs to create space to *be*. This is all about presence and becoming aware in the moment about how you are impacting your own ability to achieve. It's also how you are impacting those around you due to your behaviour. Most leaders find this the most difficult space to create, as it demands that the leader does nothing apart from being present in the moment.

Mindfulness

There are many ways that we can create space and time to think. One of these techniques is mindfulness, which is simply a way of practising to create space and time for us to think about nothing. It is a way of becoming present in the moment and noticing when our mind wanders. Practising mindfulness can be useful in helping leaders to take time out to think about what is important. When practised over time, it can also help leaders to think before speaking or making key decisions.

EXERCISE: Mindfulness

The following simple mindfulness exercise will only take five minutes. Read through the next few paragraphs to understand what is required of you and then have a go. You just need to follow the principles. Don't worry if you don't connect to the practice straight away.

For this exercise, find a quiet, peaceful space and lie down on the floor or sit in a chair or on a cushion. Try to ensure that as many parts of your body are touching the chair or floor as possible. With your eyes open, just become aware of your surroundings – the noises, the light and how your body feels in this position. Notice where your body is in contact with whatever is supporting you. Be aware of the weight in your body and feel the contact that your legs and feet have with the floor or the chair. Place your hands on your legs and lower your shoulders into a relaxed position.

Now start to notice your breath. Breathe in and out normally and feel the rhythm. Don't try to change the rhythm, just note it. Close your eyes and move your attention to the top of your head. Feel the sensation in the top of your head. Don't try to change it. Just be aware of it. Then scan down your body, noticing the feelings in your face, your shoulders, your chest, your stomach, your bottom, your legs, your ankles, your feet and, finally, your toes. Really wiggle those toes.

Now move your attention to your breath again. Start to count your breaths. Breathe in through your nose (count 1) and out through your mouth (count 2). Do this in your natural rhythm until you count to 10, and then start again at 1. As you count your breaths, notice when your mind wanders. Let it wander. Don't judge or analyse the thought. Let it come and go and then come back to counting your breaths. The mind will wander and this is OK. Just acknowledge the thought, let it go, bring your attention back to your breath and count 1 in through the nose and 2 out through the mouth.

After five minutes, move your attention back to your surroundings, hearing the noises around you and sensing the light around you. When you are ready, slowly open your eyes and move about in your seat or on the floor.

It is normal for leaders not to see much value in their early mindfulness sessions, but when practised regularly it becomes easier to create the space and time needed to think deeply about what is happening right now and what is important to you right now. The reason it takes time is that our brains are not used to working in this way. We need to build new habits in the way our minds work over time.

Once you become more effective at creating space to think about what is important to you, the next step is to support your team in creating a culture where thinking more deeply about what they do becomes a habit.

There are many mindfulness exercises available on the internet. I particularly enjoy the variety of short mindfulness exercises on the mobile app 'Headspace'.

The Ten Components of a Thinking Environment

In her book *Time to Think: Listening to ignite the human mind*[32] Nancy Kline discusses what she terms 'The Ten Components of a Thinking Environment'. These lead to better decision-making in organisations. If a leader can establish these, they will inspire other team members to think more deeply and contribute more effectively to the team:

1. **Attention**: Listening with respect, interest and fascination.

2. **Incisive questions:** These remove assumptions that limit ideas.

3. **Equality:** Treating others as thinking peers, giving equal time and attention and keeping agreements and boundaries.

4. **Appreciation:** Practising a five-to-one ratio of appreciation to criticism.

5. **Ease:** Offering freedom from rush or urgency.

6. **Encouragement:** Moving beyond competition.

---

32 N Kline, *Time to Think: Listening to ignite the human mind* (Octopus Publishing Group, 1998)

7. **Feelings:** Allowing sufficient emotional release to restore thinking.

8. **Information:** Providing a full and accurate picture of reality.

9. **Place:** Creating a physical environment that says to people, 'You matter.'

10. **Diversity:** Adding quality because of the differences between us.

With Kline's ten components in mind, what is it that you can do differently to create space for you and your team so that you can make more informed and considered decisions in your meetings?

Chapter summary

- 80% of leaders don't create enough time to think about their future organisation or key relationship needs.

- It is not easy to create space in our lives. Most leaders struggle to move from doing, to thinking and being.

- Creating space to think enables leaders to improve personal and professional performance over time.

- Creating space to think is simple, but needs discipline and focus. It becomes easier if you ask for support from those around you.

- Creating space to think enables the important things to emerge with clarity.

- Practise mindfulness and stick with it over time. Be kind to yourself as you practise.

- Encourage your team to think more deeply about what they are doing by sharing the ten principles discussed in *Time To Think*.

Actions

- Think about the next couple of weeks in your life and look for opportunities where you can create some thinking time.

- Create a list of events that you choose to no longer attend.

- Think about the four types of space you can create around thinking, connecting, doing and being.

- Think about how you can create a culture that promotes time to think.

- Ask others to support you as you practise changing your behaviours.

Amy's actions

Action notes from coaching session
Creating space
I can cancel five meetings in my diary which will
release six hours this week. I will make sure that
nothing else goes in place of those meetings and will
use the extra time to just think.
4 types of space
Thinking - not enough, will do more
Connecting - not enough with key stakeholders
Doing - lots of this but not all essential tasks
Being - need to get better at being present
Time to think
I am going to change how we run our weekly
meetings and rotate the chair. We will have more
time on the agenda to think.

PART THREE
REGENERATE

9
Resilience

Amy was walking in her local woods reflecting on a strategic away day she had led for her team the previous day. It had become clear from the deep insight gained on the day that her team were worried about the future of the organisation. They had also questioned whether they had the agility to cope with the necessary changes that needed to happen in the coming months.

Amy's coach had helpfully introduced the concept of resilience in her recent coaching session. She had to ensure that she was ready to cope with the challenging months ahead and building her resilience was going to be critical to her success. She had learned that resilience was much more than being tough. She had been encouraged to build on the skills she had been developing in recent months and needed to take her team with her in the coming months.

In any stage of your career, it is critical to focus on building and maintaining your resilience to enable you to achieve your short- and long-term goals but many leaders choose not to. They decide to work as hard as they can each day to cope with whatever is thrown at them and role-model a heroic leadership style instead.

According to the Tallents Partnership survey, 80% of respondents felt that they had improved their resilience during the pandemic, but this is an exceptional circumstance and resilience is more often misunderstood and rarely occurs consistently in leaders.

Why many leaders' resilience is inconsistent

As with any of us, varying energy levels can affect a leader's mood swings and self-confidence levels throughout the day, impacting on their clarity and consistency of decision-making. Many leaders are not aware of changes in their energy levels. This leads to inconsistent behaviour and, depending on the leader, either avoidance of conflict or the seeking out of conflict.

Many leaders are also unaware of how to schedule their day in order to maximise their effectiveness when energy levels are high; their overall personal energy management is poor. Various coping strategies for dealing with setbacks and personal failures can lead to over-optimism in some leaders, or the bounce-back effect, where a short burst of energy follows the setback. This sends team members running in all directions rather than staying focused on the long-term goal.

Leaders are also often poor at time management. They feel as though they are being effective by spending all their time in meetings and getting through their to-do lists. This leads to inconsistent decision-making on the run between meetings and a lack of availability for team members.

The benefits of building resilience

When leaders focus on building their resilience, they create time and space to think about how they feel about tasks and relationships and to manage their responses to these feelings in line with their long-term goals and purpose. Their improved self-awareness helps them to be more agile in the moment and react to challenging situations effectively.

The development of habits that encourage a more efficient management of energy levels leads to better wellbeing. Leaders can also learn how to become more present in relationships and at key moments in their day-to-day leadership responsibilities. This leads to more engaged leaders who are more aware of their impact on others in the moment.

Defining resilience

In her book *The Resilience Dynamic: The simple, proven approach to high performance and wellbeing*, Jenny Campbell defines resilience as 'your ability to adapt. It's your capacity for change.'[33] The higher your resilience is, the more agile you will be in leading and adapting to the ever-changing landscape that challenges you each day. Understanding your own resilience levels encourages you to explore your own self-awareness and how you can draw on all the internal and external resources you have open to you in the moment when it really matters. This enables you to make better decisions more often without thinking too much about how you are making them.

A common misconception about resilience is that it's getting back up and bouncing back when someone or something knocks you down in terms of confidence or failure. Campbell's book demonstrates that resilience is not about being tough and thick-skinned, or proving that you can take what people throw at you. It is much more about creating options for yourself that draw on all the resources you have available to you in the moment. She points out that resilience is not about becoming a control freak and that driving efficiency only takes a leader part of the way to higher performance; doing more in less time does not always lead to better decision-making.

---

33 J Campbell, *The Resilience Dynamic: The simple, proven approach to high performance and wellbeing* (Practical Inspiration Publishing, 2019)

The Resilience River©

A helpful way to think about resilience is through Campbell's The Resilience River®.[34] Think about a fast-flowing river that you are familiar with. A full and fast-flowing river is you with high resilience and gaining breakthrough moments. You don't have time to worry about the rocks and branches and other obstacles in the river. You are focusing on the flow of the river and adapting your position to ensure that you remain safe and effective. You are instinctively using your experience and resources in the moment and accessing self-awareness to adapt to your surroundings with maximum effect.

A slower-flowing and less energetic river is you when your resilience is lower and you are performing at a 'coping' level. As you flow down the river, you notice rocks and boulders that you haven't noticed before. Your focus is drawn to them and they seem more important than moving down the river. You become less present and self-aware of your surroundings because you are focused on the minor distractions at the bottom of the river and therefore not as aware of what is happening in the moment. This is a useful way for us to become more conscious of our resilience levels throughout the day.

---

34 J Campbell, 'The Resilience River©', © The Resilience Engine, www.resiliencengine.com (AoEC, 2021), www.aoec.com/knowledge-bank/resilience-river, accessed 23 September 2021

Resilience enablers

There are key enabling factors that can assist leaders to be resilient consistently. Campbell and The Resilience Engine refer to them as 'resilience enablers'[35] and suggest four to start with:

1. The first is practising being present. Don't think about the past or the future or what people might be thinking about you at this moment. Just experience the moment and feel what it means for you and how you are impacting others. This enables you to act appropriately in the moment and can lead to breakthroughs.

2. The second is maximising your energy when you need to be at your best. The four dimensions of energy cover mental, emotional, spiritual and physical energies. This means it is important to look after your own mental wellbeing and practise managing your own emotions. Spiritual energy is personal to you and is about connection with something bigger than you. Physical energy can be gained with the right amount of sleep each night, a balanced diet, getting and keeping fit and removing draining activities and people from your life. All of these together help you maximise your energy to be at your best and give

---

35 'Resilience enablers', © The Resilience Engine, www.resiliencengine. com

yourself the best possible chance of reacting to situations in the most effective way.

3. Thirdly, creating time and space to reflect on your decisions and relationships, to learn more about yourself and become more self-aware of how you impact your own decision-making and that of others in your team.

4. Finally, but most importantly, reconnecting with your purpose in the current environment to ensure it is still relevant and that others understand it completely. With clear purpose, decision-making in the moment becomes easier as it is clear at a subconscious level whether there is alignment with purpose or not. This enables flow and will create more breakthrough moments.

As with many enablers, the combination of these factors will create the most power. For example, you may have clear purpose and presence and be good at learning from your mistakes, but if you don't have the energy to act on the learning then you will remain stagnant until you find the energy to push forward.

Chapter summary

- Resilience is not about being tough. It's your ability to adapt and your capacity for change.

- 80% of leaders felt they improved their resilience levels during the pandemic but it is still important to focus on building our resilience even when not in crisis mode.

- Many leaders misunderstand what resilience is and mismanage their energy levels on a regular basis.

- Leaders can learn how to cope on a daily basis, but these coping strategies can become habits that inhibit long-term success.

- Building resilience leads to higher performance levels and a sense of wellbeing.

- The four resilience enablers help build our resilience levels on a daily basis leading to more breakthrough moments.

- It is important to ask for support in fulfilling your purpose and giving you the space to build your resilience over time through reflection and learning.

Actions

- Think about the next couple of weeks in your life.

- Make a real effort to be present in your key relationships in your life. Ask for support and feedback on how you are becoming more present.

- Put time in your diary each day to reflect on your activities and relationships. What can you learn from today that you can act on tomorrow to help build your resilience?

- Think about the four resilience enablers and reflect on where you are in regard to each one. Give yourself a score between 1 and 10 for each enabler. 1 represents that it is completely missing from your life at the moment and 10 means you have it present all the time. Add up your scores and evaluate on a weekly basis.

- Finally, Reconnect with who you are and why you are here, bringing further clarity to your purpose in life.

Amy's actions

Action notes from coaching session
Resilience
I am going to ask one of my team members to support me as I focus on building my resilience levels.
I tend to float between coping and breakeven most days but have noticed that I achieve breakthroughs when my energy levels are high. These tend to be highest in the mornings after I have been to the gym.
Resilience enablers
Being present-4 out of 10
Maximising energy levels-6 out of 10
Creating space and time-7 out of 10
Reconnecting with purpose-6 out of 10

10
Mental Fitness

Amy was eight months into her new role and had developed strong resilience to cope with the many change programmes that she was leading. Her leadership was tested daily and there were occasions when she doubted her ability and negative thoughts affected the clarity of her decision-making. Amy's coach encouraged her to keep a journal of negative thoughts and look for patterns around when they occurred and any recurring themes.

It was hard work, but Amy focused on turning irrational negative thoughts into positive thoughts created from her newly-discovered sage perspective. Two weeks later, her team started to give her feedback that she seemed more at ease and calmer when dealing with difficult situations. The team and her key stakeholders were confident in her ability to do the right thing, and most of all, they trusted her because she acted in a consistent manner.

It is critical to understand what your current levels of mental fitness are and times when these levels are low as they can hold you back from fulfilling your leadership potential. In a recent survey of global leaders undertaken by the Tallents Partnership, 36% of respondents stated that they did not have consistently high levels of mental fitness as they tackled their daily leadership challenges.

Mental fitness is a state of mind that ensures we feel in tip-top shape and our positive attitudes flow in the right direction. Mental fitness has little to do with intelligence or IQ tests and a lot more to do with positive thinking and affirmations. The benefits that can come from high levels of mental fitness include better sleep, lower anxiety levels and higher self-confidence.

Why many leaders have poor levels of mental fitness

Many leaders have become successful during their careers by fuelling their ability to be judgmental of others, enabling them to be decisive in the moment. This can lead to short-term success, but their decisions are usually derived from a negative mindset. Negative mindsets are often derived from deeper fears that have been held since childhood and are buried in the subconscious mind. Many leaders suffer from imposter syndrome and have low levels of self-confidence in their ability to explore their deepest fears as it calls for strong self-discipline and emotional strength. This leads to further self-doubt and the avoidance of situations that bring the fears front and centre.

Other important decision-makers in the business begin to lose confidence in the leader as they feel disengaged and discouraged due to the leader's behaviour. Not enough leaders are challenged by others to confront these beliefs, and leaders rarely challenge themselves to think deeply about how these beliefs and fears might be holding them back.

Many leaders also make incorrect assumptions about their ability to deal with difficult people and situations. They tend to remember the bad outcomes and this reinforces their fears. They forget the situations they have managed effectively and don't ask for feedback on when they have been effective. They also make the assumption that their various stakeholders don't notice the behaviours that are linked to their self-limiting beliefs or fears, but as leaders are in the spotlight and their behaviours are amplified, patterns of behaviour soon emerge. The stakeholders simply learn how to manage the leader's dysfunctionality to the extent that the problem often goes away until a critical situation arises and the behaviour needs to be addressed by one of the parties involved. All too often, leaders are not incentivised to address their poor mental fitness levels.

Building your own mental fitness

Once a leader understands how to change their negative thoughts into positive thoughts, it can lead to opportunities for further personal development. For example, a leader who previously believed that they were not effective at public speaking can change their internal beliefs and find opportunities to represent their organisation in public forums. With further practice, they can develop their broader communication skills in the process.

The five Sage Powers

In his book *Positive Intelligence: Why only 20% of teams and individuals achieve their true potential and how you can achieve yours*,[36] Shirzad Chamine talks about the five powers of our 'inner sage' that enable leaders to turn negative thoughts into positive thoughts and improve mental fitness. Chamine's brief description of each power is as follows:

1. **Empathise:** Be kind to yourself and others. See the inner child within yourself and others and become aware of the essence of the person you are in a relationship with. When we have negative thoughts about others, it helps to put

---

36 S Chamine, *Positive Intelligence: Why only 20% of teams and individuals achieve their true potential and how you can achieve yours* (Greenleaf Book Group, 2012)

ourselves in their shoes and look at relationship issues from their perspective.

2. **Explore:** Become a keen observer of what simply is, without any other influence over the situation. It's difficult to not judge, change or try to control what's going on. Try to discover things exactly as they are, without a selective filter.

3. **Innovate:** Follow every new idea you or others have by saying, 'Yes, what I love about that idea is… and…' With this approach, every idea is appreciated rather than judged before the next thought is generated in reaction to it. The key is rapid succession – whether played in your head or in a team setting.

4. **Navigate:** When faced with a fork in the road, imagine yourself at the end of your life looking back at the choices you are now facing. From that perspective, what do you wish you had chosen at this juncture? At the end of our lives, many of our concerns driven by negative thoughts fall away and reveal themselves as false.

5. **Activate:** By becoming more self-aware of when negative thoughts arise, you can begin to predict when they are about to appear and prepare an action plan that moves you from negative thinking into action and positive thinking.

This needs practice and support from others in helping you move towards positive action.[37]

These five powers can help leaders to think more positively about their key relationships and how they feel about themselves. When leaders make decisions from a positive perspective, these tend to be more informed and considered decisions that lead to longer-term success.

Self-limiting beliefs

When I ask my clients to list some of their self-limiting beliefs and to think about what they believe they are not good at, or situations where they are self-critical about themselves, these are some common responses:

- *'I need to keep adding value.'* Many leaders have a self-limiting belief that they must always be seen to be adding value to everything they do. Unfortunately, this can be counterproductive at times, particularly when others in the organisation are better equipped to add the value required. If a leader can change this belief, it allows them to focus on what the team needs rather than just adding value. Often, when we explore what lies behind this belief, new self-awareness emerges around how previous

---

37 'Sage Power Games', Positive Intelligence, no date, https://support. positiveintelligence.com/article/143-power-games

negative experiences of feeling under-valued have reinforced the belief and we can focus on future behaviours to replace past behaviours.

- *'I need to be the smartest person in the room.'* Many leaders feel they need to show that they have the highest IQ in the room to bolster their position in relation to decision-making. The reality is that there will be people in the room smarter than the leader and they will tend to be able to question the leader in such a way that demonstrates this. If a leader can show their vulnerability by saying they don't know all the answers, then they are more likely to gain the support of their team.

- *'I need to retain control.'* Many leaders believe that if they don't retain control of the way their team behaves, they won't be able to deliver against their personal objectives. This belief leads to micromanagement and a lack of trust within the team. When we explore what lies behind this belief, self-awareness emerges about previous negative experiences where the leader felt helpless and out of control. They ensure that this does not happen again by gaining a position of authority where they can retain control.

- *'I need to lead from a position of strength.'* Many leaders have seen role models demonstrate heroic leadership focused on playing to their strengths and not being open about their weaknesses. This lack of vulnerability can lead to stress and anxiety for the leader as they fail to recognise how their weaknesses hold them back.

- *'I need to win at all costs.'* Many leaders have a competitive side to them and want to prove themselves worthy of the leadership role they have taken on. Depending on the company culture, this can be unhealthy for other team members as values are compromised and the leader's behaviour becomes aligned to winning at all costs. When the leader wins, others in the wider system tend to lose. This is a complex self-limiting belief and tends to be linked to events from the leader's childhood.

Managing your limiting self-beliefs

In becoming more aware of the reasons behind their beliefs, leaders can change their behaviour and become more inclusive in their decision-making by looking for win/win outcomes.

Once you start to become more aware of your self-limiting beliefs, you can explore real evidence that either supports or rejects the belief. The table below shows examples of real self-limiting beliefs and sentences of evidence that either support or contradict the belief.

Self-limiting belief	Evidence for belief	Evidence against belief
I need to be in control.	When I let go, it tends to go wrong.	I delegated a key task last week and it went well.
Nobody respects me.	The team answers me back.	The team gives me positive feedback.
I can't do presentations.	I always get caught out by unexpected questions.	I present at least once a week to various audiences.
I can't manage conflict.	I get frustrated and angry.	I manage conflict better in groups.
I can't do the detail.	I miss important facts I need to know.	I can do detail if I create the space and focus.

EXERCISE: Identify your self-limiting beliefs

Take a few minutes to draw your own table like the one above.

Think about what comes to mind when you start a sentence with:

- 'I need...'
- 'I can't...'
- 'I am not good at...'
- 'I always...'

List a few of your own self-limiting beliefs in the first column. In the second column, write as many sentences as you can that provide evidence to support each self-limiting belief. In the third column, write as many sentences as you can that provide evidence that might challenge the belief.

A common self-limiting belief is 'I am not good at managing conflict', causing people to avoid conflict situations as much as possible. As a leader, it is inevitable that conflict situations will arise as you hold others to account. In this example, you might evidence that when you have to deal with conflict in the moment, the outcome shows that you do not handle the situation effectively. You could also have evidence that you deal with conflict effectively when you have time to prepare so, in this case, working out a coping strategy that allows you to delay the surprise conflict situation until the next day will be effective. You have the right not to deal with the situation in the moment, and can explain that it is more appropriate to deal with it when both parties are calmer. You will feel more confident after preparing for the conflict situation. This will benefit both parties, as the outcome will usually be more effective.

By considering the evidence for and against our self-limiting beliefs, we can engineer coping strategies to help us build confidence in overcoming those beliefs – but these are only coping strategies.

Fear

Behind every self-limiting belief is usually a deeper, subconscious fear. Once leaders begin to understand and cope with their self-limiting beliefs, they can start to explore their fears. The table below lists some of the most common fears that leaders tend to have.

Fear	Behaviour	Outcome
Failure	Risk-averse	Lost opportunities
Not being liked	Avoid making unpopular decisions	Unresolved people issues
Looking stupid	Pretending I have the answers when I don't	Inauthentic leadership and loss of self-confidence
Conflict	Avoid difficult discussions	Unresolved people issues
Being found out	Keep my head down	Sub-optimal performance

The more courageous a leader can be in identifying and facing their fears, the more effective they will become over time. In everyday work situations, most of the fears that leaders have are completely irrational, and yet we all feel them to a certain extent. These fears inhibit certain behaviours and stop leaders from fulfilling their potential.

In my coaching sessions, the leader will list their fears and then think deeply about the behaviour that the fear drives. They can then work out the likely consequences of their behaviour. For example, if a leader has a fear of failure, they may adopt strategies that are more likely to be successful in the short term, rather than take risks that could lead to failure in the short term but success in the long term because of the learnings gained by failing. Once the leader understands the range of consequences that can occur if they don't overcome their fear, they can make a more informed decision on whether the fear needs to be addressed.

EXERCISE: Identify your fear behaviours

Take five minutes to become more aware of your own fears and the behaviours that they drive. Create a table like the one above and list your fears, the behaviours that the fear drives, and the possible consequences of that behaviour.

Commit to a single action which can move you closer to overcoming one of your irrational fears that will affect your long-term success.

How to overcome your fears

There are many proven techniques to help leaders overcome their fears.

Neuro-Linguistic Programming (NLP): Our minds receive information through our senses, but the emotional impact of that information depends on whether we mentally associate or disassociate with it. We associate by viewing and experiencing an event through our bodies. We are literally in the experience, processing it from the perspective of, 'I see, feel and hear this event.' We disassociate by taking an 'other' perspective, as if we are an observer outside of our bodies. In other words, 'I'm watching myself going through this experience.' Associated experiences have a more powerful emotional impact than disassociated experiences because we are attached rather than detached. It's the difference between imagining yourself looking out of the front car of a rollercoaster as you speed around the track or viewing an image of yourself at a distance taking the ride.

Understanding this difference in perspectives can be useful in helping leaders overcome fears or past traumatic experiences. Richard Bandler, co-creator of NLP, developed a desensitisation technique that can be performed in less than ten minutes. The process helps clients to safely confront their fears by disassociating and reframing their experience. It is useful to understand how NLP might be able to help you overcome any deep fears that are holding you back as a leader. You can find out more information about NLP at https://richardbandler.com

Cognitive Behavioural Therapy (CBT): CBT enables you to manage your fears by helping you gradually change the way you think. It's based on the interconnectedness of thoughts, beliefs, feelings and behaviours. It may take several CBT sessions to counteract a certain thought pattern. To accomplish this, you can overcome your fear with incremental steps. For example, a sample plan to address a fear of dogs might include first reading about dogs, then watching a dog movie and finally, going to play with a friend's harmless puppy. Techniques commonly used in CBT draw from the schools of behaviourism and learning theory, as well as the school of cognitive theory.

Gestalt therapy: Gestalt therapy focuses on process (what is actually happening) over content (what is being talked about). The emphasis is on what is being done, thought and felt at the present moment rather than on what was, might be, could be or should have been. It is a method of awareness practice where the distinction between direct experience vs indirect (or secondary) interpretation is developed during therapy. Becoming aware of what they are doing triggers a client's ability to risk a shift or change in behaviour.

Professional therapy: Professional therapists can experiment with different approaches using their professional training to support the leader to overcome their deep-rooted fears. Therapists who specialise in personal trauma can use a psychodynamic approach to enable the leader to explore their subconscious for any childhood experiences that could explain the reasons that lie behind their fears.

Defeating our Saboteurs

Although all of the therapies highlighted above are worthwhile considering, they all require the involvement of a third party. An innovative way of overcoming many of the negative thoughts driven by our fears was designed by Shirzad Chamine in 2012. In his book *Positive Intelligence: Why only 20% of teams and individuals achieve their true potential and how you can achieve yours,* as well as the five Sage Powers that can help us move towards more positive thinking,[38] Chamine also explains that we all have powerful Saboteurs that love to nurture negative thoughts every minute of the day.

The Judge and Accomplice Saboteurs

As children, we learn to survive our family and education systems by creating stories that make us feel better about the situations in which we find ourselves. The main story that we create as children is that it is OK to judge other people so we can protect ourselves. Chamine calls this aspect of our personality 'the Judge'. We know the Judge is present whenever we experience a negative thought. The Judge causes much of our disappointment, anger, regret, guilt, shame and anxiety. We judge ourselves when the inner critic is loud in our minds. We judge others when we have negative thoughts about how someone behaves or

---

38 www.positiveintelligence.com/assessments

makes us feel. We judge the situations we find ourselves in when we feel unloved, victimised or that life is just not fair. Chamine explains that:

> 'Saboteurs start off as our guardians to help us survive the real and imagined threats to our physical and emotional survival as children. By the time we are adults, we no longer need them, but they have become invisible inhabitants of our mind.'[39]

The Judge usually gains some help from one or more of these 'Accomplice' Saboteurs to help cement our negativity. When we have a positive mindset, the Saboteurs are quiet and our natural inner strengths are in flow. When we are thinking negatively, the Saboteurs restrict our ability to perform effectively and reduce our leadership potential. This is a list of the nine Saboteurs that Chamine refers to, along with a brief description:

1. **The Stickler** insists on perfection, order and organisation.

2. **The Pleaser** indirectly tries to gain acceptance and affection by helping, pleasing, rescuing or flattering others. Loses sight of own needs and becomes resentful as a result.

3. **The Hyper-achiever** is dependent on constant performance and achievement for self-respect

---

39 S. Chamine, *Positive Intelligence*

and self-validation. Highly focused on external success, leading to unsustainable workaholic tendencies and loss of touch with deeper emotional and relationship needs.

4. **The Victim** tends to be emotional and temperamental to gain attention and affection. There is an extreme focus on internal feelings, particularly painful ones. Martyr streak.

5. **The Hyper-rational** intensely focuses on the rational processing of everything, including relationships. Can be perceived as cold, distant and intellectually arrogant.

6. **The Hyper-vigilant** anxiously focuses on everything that could go wrong. Vigilance that can never rest.

7. **The Restless** constantly searches for greater excitement in the next activity or through constant busyness. Rarely at peace or content with the current activity.

8. **The Controller** has an anxiety-based need to take charge and control situations and people's actions to one's own will. They experience high anxiety and impatience when that is not possible.

9. **The Avoider** focuses on the positive and pleasant to the extreme and avoids difficult and unpleasant tasks and conflicts.

Once we become more self-aware of which Saboteurs are supporting our Judge when we have negative feelings or thoughts, we can choose to think differently using the five Sage Powers. Take a moment to look through the list of Saboteurs. Which two or three can you relate to the most? Which ones are most present when you have negative thoughts?

Chapter summary

- 36% of leaders don't have consistently high mental fitness levels to deal effectively with day-to-day leadership challenges.

- Many of our negative thoughts are driven by our self-limiting beliefs and fears.

- We can become more self-aware of our self-limiting beliefs by identifying evidence for and against those beliefs.

- We can become more self-aware of our fears by analysing the behaviours and outcomes that are driven by those fears.

- There are many ways to overcome our fears, but most of them require help from third-party professionals.

- High levels of mental fitness encourage positive thinking and enable us to draw on our five Sage Powers.

- Understanding more about the Judge and the Accomplice Saboteurs can help us manage our negative feelings more effectively over time and can also help us overcome our fears.

Actions

- Think about the next couple of weeks in your life and look for opportunities where you can create some thinking time.

- Create a list of self-limiting beliefs and fears.

- Think about the outcomes that could be achieved if you changed your beliefs.

- Keep a journal for a week and make a note every time you have a negative feeling. Identify the strongest Saboteurs that might be holding you back when you have negative feelings.

- Ask others to support you as you practise moving from negative thinking to positive thinking.

Amy's actions

Action notes from coaching session

Mental fitness

My top self-limiting beliefs are:

I don't deserve to progress until I over achieve.
I prefer people to like me than dislike me.
People are not interested in my opinions.

My deepest fears are:

Failure, Conflict and Loneliness

My top three saboteurs are:

Hyper-Achiever
Controller
Pleaser

11
Leading Teams

Amy was feeling great pride in her achievements after twelve months in the role. In her annual appraisal, she was informed that the Board had confidence in her ability to lead the transformation programme and that they trusted her leadership style would benefit the organisation in the long term. One thing in the appraisal process was troubling her, though. Carlos was worried about the depth of strength of Amy's team and he could not see a natural successor to her.

Amy had been encouraged to develop her team and embed her self-coaching skills within the team. It was fair to say that she had focused on herself in the first twelve months and was reliant on her team members to manage their own personal development. Amy worked with her coach to design a plan that would enable her to take more of a coaching leadership style with her team over the coming months.

In any stage of your career, it is critical to provide courageous and clear leadership to your team. An increasing number of leaders are discovering the benefits of using a coaching leadership style to improve the performance of their teams. This became particularly relevant during the Covid pandemic as they learned to lead remote teams more effectively.

Why leaders should develop a coaching leadership style

Many leaders choose not to coach their teams as this requires a focus on creating time for the team and planning in advance. Most leaders feel that they don't have enough time to prepare for team meetings. These meetings tend to become transactional, looking back rather than being in the present. Leaders know they need to get more out of their meetings, but never get round to thinking about it.

Once leaders understand how to develop a coaching leadership style, it can lead to opportunities for further personal development. For example, a leader who takes time out to reflect on how effective a meeting was can think about ways to improve the overall team performance in future meetings.

Understanding how to develop a coaching leadership style helps leaders to think more deeply about their team members' strengths and how to challenge them by taking them out of their comfort zone and building their self-confidence further. A leader's coaching leadership style can also set the tone for the rest of the organisation and inspire other employees to become more self-aware of how they can create the same style for their own teams.

By developing a coaching leadership style, leaders often build their self-confidence and vulnerability. This enables them to become more decisive and courageous as leaders. It also enables them to rely on their teams more often, creating more time to focus on the essential tasks and relationships that only they can manage.

Six steps to develop an effective coaching leadership style

To develop an effective coaching leadership style, you need to show that you are aware of the strengths and weaknesses of your teams and, with the support of others around you, that you are willing to change your own leadership habits accordingly. I usually work in six areas or steps of team coaching with my clients. How many you choose to work on, and where you begin in the process, will depend on where you are currently with your team:

Step 1: Weekly leadership meetings

The first step is how a leader can make weekly leadership team meetings as productive as possible. Most leaders have similar agendas: they review the previous week and then discuss the coming week's potential problems and opportunities. Leaders need to take time to think about what needs to change to gain better outcomes. These prompts can assist with this:

- Think about the purpose of the meeting. What needs to change about this?

- Clearly communicate the purpose of the meeting and what outcomes you are looking for to the team.

- Prior to the meeting, provide information to the team that will help them achieve the desired outcome. Make it clear that each team member is expected to read the information prior to the meeting so that they can fully utilise the time available to them.

- Where could you delegate the role of chair to another team member? (Most leaders who try this are pleased to have a rest from this.)

- Consider rotating the role among each team member. Although each team member can chair the meeting in their own way, the purpose and expected outcomes are still clearly stated by the leader and the chair is held accountable by the team.

- Finally, try and create a coaching leadership style within the dynamics of the meeting and an environment that encourages team members to think more deeply and make more informed and considered decisions in team meetings. (Refer to The Ten Components in Chapter 8.)

How might this look in practice? The chair of the meeting states the purpose of the meeting and the ideal outcome the team is working towards. For example, 'The purpose of the meeting is to better understand how customers are responding to our new product/service in the market. Our ideal outcome is to make a decision on what changes need to be made to this product/service in the coming weeks.'

The chair asks that each team member say in turn, without being interrupted or challenged, what is going well at the moment. Once the team member has finished speaking, other team members ask incisive questions to reveal and remove any assumptions that limit ideas. The team then breaks into thinking partnership pairs. Each person in the pair thinks out loud for five minutes without interruption before they all regroup as a team. Each team member then gets another turn to speak without interruption in relation to the purpose and desired outcome of the meeting.

Throughout the meeting, the chair encourages the sharing of truth and relevant information, and also encourages the expression of feelings that others are not openly allowed to judge. The chair summarises what they have heard and how this informs the decisions that need to be made. The normal team decision-making process can then take place. To conclude the meeting, the chair asks everyone what they think went well in the meeting and what they respect in one another.

Even though the format of this meeting is different to meetings that normally take place, it does encourage high-quality thinking. It also provides a broader perspective, as more views are shared from within the group. Leaders often think that this kind of meeting will take longer than their normal meetings, but in practice, giving team members more quality time to think and building on others' ideas and thoughts makes the meeting more productive in the long term. Other variations around this theme can be experimented with by the leader until they are happy with the output.

Step 2: Team discovery days

The second step is understanding the current team dynamics and raising the whole team's awareness of each others' preferred working styles, and how to get the most from one another. Leaders don't tend to take much time to really understand their team members and how they interact with each other on a daily basis. By taking just one day out with the team, the leader can share information with them gained from psychometric profiles that will enable the team members to raise their own self-awareness of how they behave, and what this tends to mean for the team dynamic. There are many psychometric profiling tools on the market, but one that measures emotional intelligence will give the best indication of a team member's appetite for changing their own behaviours. This helps team members to work out how they tend to behave, why they behave like they do, and where their emotional intelligence levels are currently. Offsite away days allow the team to bond in a different setting and team members can be more open about what they need from their colleagues. Successful team days encourage vulnerability and openness, and result in the team feeling closer and more understanding of one another.

Once team members understand their own behaviour traits and why they behave as they do, they may want to commit to changing their behaviours in relation to other key team members, for example, being less dominant around people or listening more. Whatever the behaviour change, working with an executive coach might help team members to change their behaviour over time. If the coach is effective, the team will make more demands of their leader in giving them feedback and challenging them more on a daily basis. Leaders can accelerate this behaviour change by adopting a coaching leadership style.

Once the team members are working more effectively together, there may be opportunities for the leader to coach a particular relationship. This involves acting as an independent third party, observing behaviours that are present in the relationship, and coaching each team member in how they may be able to make positive changes in the relationship. This is an effective technique, but needs the leader to listen, engage and advise in equal measure.

Step 3: Creating team values, vision and purpose

Once team dynamics have been improved and the team becomes more effective at working together, they need to understand what they are working towards as a team. Many companies are able to produce their own purpose and values statements, but these are often misunderstood and don't always translate well to the leadership teams that need to follow them. It is often necessary for the team to develop their own purpose and vision, a statement that helps them to perform at their highest levels while operating within the wider organisation's purpose and values. Leaders can play a key role in developing their team's own purpose and values, one that each team member feels they helped to create and own more easily going forward.

Leaders can run half-day workshops to help the team understand more fully where the organisation's purpose and value statements came from so that they become easier to relate to. Leaders can then encourage each team member to identify their own purpose and values through creative exercises that take the team members out of their comfort zones. These are presented back by each team member and then a creative team session (ideally using The Ten Components in Chapter 8) works on identifying the purpose and values of the team. Once these have been established, it is important to gain buy-in from each team member. The leader must also design the accountability framework by which each team member will hold each other to account and live the purpose and values of the team.

Step 4: Team dysfunctionality

Once the team is more aware of each other and they have clarity of team purpose and values, they are ready to develop an awareness of the current dysfunctions that exist within the team. Patrick Lencioni's work in this area is powerful in moving teams towards being high-performing. By talking openly about each of the phases of team development within the Trust Pyramid discussed in Chapter 6, the team can move through the various levels of the pyramid to become high-performing.

Step 5: Systemic team coaching disciplines

The fifth step is for leaders to develop a systemic team coaching approach that takes into account external factors outside of the team. As the team becomes more effective and self-aware, they start to realise that there are external forces in play which are difficult to identify. They need to start to understand the system they are operating within.

We all work in various systems. One of the earliest systems we become aware of is our family system. We learn the rules and the behaviours of the people in the system and we work out ways to survive or thrive. We work out our place in educational systems and this also affects our behaviour. We then move into our first organisation and encounter another system, etc. The team needs to learn and respect the different forces that are in play in the system so that they can perform as effectively as possible.

In 1990, Peter Hawkins began developing the systemic team coaching model. He identified five key areas, or 'disciplines' for leaders to work with, depending on the needs of their team at the time. For the model to be effective, 'teams need to have mastered all five disciplines and… systemic team coaches, and team leaders, need to be able to coach teams both within each discipline and on the connections between these disciplines.'[40]

1. **Commissioning discipline:** If the team is not clear what is expected of them, the leader needs to lead a team session to gain clarity about informal and formal performance targets (eg, Brighton & Hove Albion football team need to clearly understand what the board expects from them in terms of the number of points that need to be gained in the Premier League). If boards or owners avoid setting clear expectations then the team will need to put themselves in their paymaster's shoes and create a range of expectations that they can share with their stakeholders. This is an important factor in systemic team coaching. The leadership team can be highly effective, but if they are not giving the shareholders or board directors what they need, they will be seen as failures in the long term.

2. **Connecting discipline:** Another important factor operating within the system are the various stakeholders that have an interest in the success of the leadership team. This is where the connecting discipline is so important. The leader creates an environment where the team identifies as many of their key stakeholders as possible,

---

40 Henley Business School, 'Insight Guide #6 - How can I coach my team?' (Henley Business School, no date), www.henley.fi/app/uploads/2019/05/INSIGHT-GUIDE-No-6-online-How-can-I-coach-my-team.pdf

and creatively works out how each stakeholder feels about the way the team is operating (eg, the team may be successful in creating a profitable range of products that regularly win awards and surpass recognised industry technical standards, but if the customers don't like the way the products are being distributed, the products are likely to underperform in the market). By gaining an understanding of the various positions that stakeholders take during the year, the team can gain real insight and change their behaviours or team approach accordingly.

3. **Co-creating discipline**: This has similarities with understanding team dynamics, but also includes the assignment of roles within the team (not just in terms of functional roles, but roles to help the team become even more effective in achieving its goals).

4. **Clarifying discipline**: This is similar to the work around creating purpose and values within the team, but it also determines the way in which the team is going to measure itself against its objectives. This will include KPIs and the ways in which they will be held to account by others.

5. **Capturing the core learning:** Finally, the way that the team keeps moving to become high-performing is by developing an internal process for capturing the core learning from the insight gained from the first four disciplines. The leader teaches the team to self-coach in meetings

and in daily interactions, taking into account all the systemic elements. Over time this becomes a successful habit and a natural way of behaving.

There is never a good time to begin systemic team coaching. In reality, it is normal for team members to come and go. Many leaders want to wait until the team is more stable, but it is better to accept that the team is dynamic and understanding the system is the best way to gain high performance over time. Successful systemic team coaching programmes tend to take place over a two-year period, but the time invested leads to more effective high-performing teams in the long term.

Step 6: Ongoing leadership team coaching

Once the team has explored systemic coaching, the challenge for the leader is to coach the team dynamic on a daily basis so that the natural intelligence that exists within the team system emerges at the right time and the team stays in flow. Much of the role of the leader is to notice blockages and obstacles that stop the natural flow of information and intelligence within the team. Sometimes the obstacles are created by dysfunctional team members and sometimes the blockages are naturally created by the success or failure of the team.

This stage of the coaching leadership approach is the most demanding and requires exceptional self-leadership and high emotional intelligence levels. The leader needs to have developed themselves through the three stages of the self-coaching cycle to be able to sustain these high levels of performance within the team. The road to developing a high-performing team is challenging, complex and uncertain. Leaders can maximise their chances of success if they consistently work on their individual self-coaching with disciplined self-leadership. This will give them the confidence to coach their team effectively, which then builds confidence within the team. The leader can set more demanding objectives for the team that will stretch them further over time. To sustain this success, the leader will also need to demonstrate courageous and vulnerable leadership so that team members can learn how to become more courageous and vulnerable themselves.

Chapter summary

- Many leaders choose not to develop a coaching leadership style as it takes time and planning to become effective.

- Become more aware of how you currently lead your team. Involve them more in your decision-making, but build accountability into how the decisions are made so that the team also feels ownership.

- Spend more time with your team to really get to know what they need from you at this time.

- Encourage your team to think more deeply about how and what they are doing. Where is the team dysfunctional? How do you as a leader contribute to that?

- Develop a core vision, purpose and common values that are unique to the team, but aligned to the company vision, purpose and values.

- Take time to explore and understand the system the team is operating in.

- Over time, develop a unique coaching leadership style that your team trusts and enables them to be in flow more often.

Actions

- Think about the next couple of weeks in your life and look for opportunities where you can lead your team differently.

- Create time to think in your weekly leadership meetings.

- Decide what support your team needs as you understand the dysfunctionality that exists within the team.

- Think about how you can sustain the team's high performance over time.

- Ask others to support you as you practise changing your behaviours.

- Take a couple of minutes to think about where you can start to coach your team more effectively. What one step can you take tomorrow to lead the team more effectively? Think about:

  - Your weekly meetings

  - The team dynamics

  - The team's purpose and values

  - Systemic team coaching

  - Sustaining the high performance of your team

Amy's actions

Action notes from coaching session
Leading teams
Developing a coaching leadership style
Need to set up an away day to focus on team purpose, vision & values
Need to ask the team to complete a Lencioni 5 dysfunctions assessment
Need a follow-up workshop to explore team dysfunctionality
Engage with a systemic team coach to help us become more aware of the system we are operating in as a team

12
Coaching Culture

Amy had been in her role for eighteen months. Her coach was confident in her ability both to self-coach, and to coach others to enable them to reach their full potential. Amy was feeling an inner strength she had never felt before and was pleasantly surprised when her coach said that she no longer needed sessions.

She had been asked to attend a meeting with the chair and the CEO and she wasn't sure about the agenda. She worked hard to manage the inner voices that were casting doubt on her future. During the meeting, they both explained that Carlos had decided to retire from the business and that they would be conducting a global search for his successor. They wanted Amy to apply for the role, but more importantly, they set her a challenge of embedding her self-coaching learning into the whole organisation. The way she went about this would contribute to evidence that would support her application. When Amy left the meeting, she got into her car and screamed with delight at the top of her voice. She knew that she now had the opportunity of a lifetime.

What coaching cultures feel like

Ultimately, the reason I do what I do is to enable leaders to experience the benefits of coaching. This inspires them to lead themselves and their teams more effectively and to teach their employees more about coaching. We can all feel a coaching culture when we are present in one.

In organisations that have created a coaching culture, you can ask anyone in the organisation what the purpose and vision of their employer is and you will get broadly consistent answers. Not only that, but they will also understand their own role in fulfilling that purpose and vision, and how their own purpose and ambition is linked to the wider organisation's goals.

When you look at how decisions are made in an organisation that has created a coaching culture, you will tend to find that decisions are made in the moment by staff at all levels with a clear understanding about who is accountable for that decision. There is also a high level of trust between leaders and their teams, and colleagues trust each other implicitly. This reduces bureaucracy and time delays in decision-making, enabling agile responses to customer service issues.

Leaders in organisations that have created a coaching culture do much listening and guiding throughout the day, with little direction being given in terms of the way things get done. They set clear expectations of deliverables and coach their teams to develop their own solutions that are aligned with the organisation's purpose, vision and values.

Within coaching cultures, employees are also constantly learning about how to maximise their contribution. They are encouraged to think about their own personal challenges, how they are going to solve them, and to take full responsibility for the consequences of their decision-making. This leads to employees learning how to self-coach over time and fulfil their own potential as human beings. This can be encouraged by creating what R Kegan terms a 'deliberately developmental organisation' in his book *An Everyone Culture: Becoming a Deliberately Developmental Organization*.[41] It enables employees to seek opportunities to stretch themselves outside of their functional expertise.

Benefits of creating a coaching culture

A coaching culture focuses on enabling the individual to identify their key development areas and strengths. Through skilled coaching, leaders create

---

41 R Kegan, *An Everyone Culture: Becoming a Deliberately Developmental Organization* (Harvard Business Review Press, 2016)

an opportunity for staff to identify personal development opportunities rather than being told where they need to develop. Research has shown that a coaching culture enables more effective change management at all levels of the organisation. Coaching employees enables them to better understand their role in driving change that is aligned with both organisational and individual purpose. Over time, the whole organisation becomes an organic and agile learning system as individuals drive their own personal development in line with the company's goals and purpose. Leadership becomes less directive and more guiding and supportive in helping to remove everyday obstacles that hinder employees in achieving their personal goals.

In an organisation that has created a coaching culture, deep democracy is developed, which encourages a wider variety of voices from across the organisation. This encourages the silent majority to air their views and opinions and the system learns more effectively from those voices rather than just listening to the vocal few.

Over time, leadership, team and individual performance improves in an organisation that has created a coaching culture. Although it is difficult to measure return on investment for coaching programmes, the best KPIs are derived from employee engagement surveys, 360-degree surveys and Net Promoter Scores.

Measuring return on investment (ROI)

Despite all of these qualitative benefits, many leaders still remain sceptical about the value of investing in the creation of a coaching culture due to the difficulty in measuring the ROI.

In the 2016 Ridler Report, E.ON UK (the German-owned utility company) was surveyed on how it measured its ROI in relation to its investment in external and internal coaching support for its employees.[42] Between January 2012 and June 2015, coaching generated an average ROI of 2,685%. This means that for every £1,000 spent on coaching, E.ON UK received a return of £26,685. This was measured in numerous ways, including reduction in the number of customer complaints and cost savings derived through the outcomes of coaching programmes. In the same report, 92% of leaders surveyed felt that coaching had helped to improve their business performance.

Another widely used KPI is the use of 360-degree feedback related to business performance indicators, for example, feedback on how much more effective the employee has been with their communication skills since receiving coaching, or dealing with conflict more effectively by resolving personal staff disputes directly rather than using management time.

---

42 Ridler & Co, 'The 6th Ridler Report', www.ridlerandco.com/ridler-report

The impact of developing a coaching culture can be maximised by nurturing internal coaching capability to support leaders as they embrace a coaching leadership style. This can lead to significant cost savings when replacing existing external coaching resources.

How to develop a coaching culture within your organisation

Leaders first need to be able to demonstrate that they are aware of their own strengths and weaknesses and are willing to change their own leadership habits with the support of those around them. The next step is to master self-leadership and to role-model a team coaching leadership style which encourages high-performance teams to emerge.

Once wider team members experience the value of coaching first-hand, it is important to provide coaching to senior leaders and middle managers so that they can understand and develop the skills needed to build confidence in their own coaching leadership style.

Leaders need to proactively develop the emotional and social intelligence of their teams. This starts with first raising self-awareness and then increasing an understanding of how team members impact one another. This finally culminates in the ability of the team members to identify and collaborate within their own group and with other teams. Once team members understand this, it is possible to develop a systemic coaching approach across the organisation. The organisation becomes a living organism, guided by its employees doing the right thing in the moment and in line with an organisation's vision, values and purpose. The final stage of the journey is enabling the employees to contribute in their own way to developing a 'deliberately developmental organisation'. The basic premise is that team members are encouraged to challenge themselves on a daily basis for both their own and the organisation's benefit.

Developing the right coaching framework

A key element in successfully developing a coaching culture is how the leader develops a coaching training framework. All of us have the innate ability to coach ourselves and others, but these skills are not actively encouraged in most organisations. Leaders need to take care in how the training is designed and delivered to ensure that participants not only learn, but practise the skills so that they become embedded in their daily habits.

Many training programmes have fantastic content and today's technology enables fast-paced learning, but there is much evidence to suggest that when we learn new skills on training programmes, we also need to practise those skills for at least three weeks for the learning to take hold and be applied naturally in our everyday lives. This enables us to form new habits in the way we coach ourselves and others.

Many organisations have talented HR teams that can provide excellent training, but I encourage leaders to benchmark their own solutions with those provided by external providers, and where possible, partner with a professional coaching training company. Even the best training organisations can't mind-read, so developing clear objectives for your training is key. The best way to think about this is envisioning the outcomes you want to achieve with effective training, for example, 'better 360-feedback on leadership style' or 'improved performance in Net Promoter Score'. Whatever your objectives are, your training partner will be better able to design the right programme. A professional training partner will test and clarify their understanding of the programme goals and will want to see consistency and clarity of thinking across the senior leadership team before committing to training delivery.

Once the training programme has been agreed, the senior leadership team needs to sponsor the training and role-model the behaviours they are looking to create within the organisation so that employees can see the importance of the training and that they need to take it seriously.

As with most training programmes, it is best to start small with teaching basic coaching skills. These include:

- Active and engaged listening
- Enabling others to have the time to think before responding to a question
- Moving from directive questioning to a position of curiosity
- Being comfortable with silence
- Creating space and time to think for themselves before responding in a relationship

These skills are best regained and practised through experiential learning, supported by some theoretical knowledge. Learning in triads enables the participants to take the part of the coach, the coachee and an observer to maximise their learning from three different perspectives. Above all, the training needs to be fun and leave the participants with actions to practise for the next three weeks. Employees will vary in their interest levels after the training, but these skills are generally useful in an employee's personal and work life. For those that are interested to learn more, there is an opportunity to provide further progression with a mix of further face-to-face practice and online learning.

Once the external training programme has concluded, most organisations develop an inhouse coaching pool that are qualified and experienced in providing support in coaching skills across the organisation to help embed the skills. Training partners can provide more in-depth programmes that include diploma qualifications approved by the International Coaching Federation.

The journey to forming new habits that enable you to develop a coaching culture within an organisation is a long and challenging adventure. There will be times when you feel you are making breakthroughs, and days when you are back to old habits. This is normal for all of us. It takes time and trust to create the environment that is so important to developing a coaching culture. Once you start role-modelling the right behaviours, you can support others who want to self-coach themselves and coach others in the organisation. Over time, every employee can learn how to support each other and organisation performance will improve.

Chapter summary

- Organisations that create coaching cultures look and feel different to most other organisations.

- There are many qualitative and quantitative benefits to creating a coaching culture within your organisation.

- Role-model a coaching leadership style. Make sure you master the discipline of self-leadership and build a self-coaching habit. Coach your relationships with others and encourage others to develop their own coaching leadership style.

- Develop a robust coaching framework so your employees feel more confident in coaching their teams. Provide them with the basic tools of active and engaged listening, the ability to create space for others to think and develop their own ideas, and the confidence to use a coaching leadership style in their own relationships.

- Encourage your employees to contribute to developing a 'deliberately developmental organisation'. Ask them to take responsibility and ownership of their own development and encourage them to ask for feedback and opportunities to stretch themselves further each day.

- Work at understanding the system your employees are operating within. This is about understanding the organisation's needs and enabling your employees to trust their own judgment and voice their feelings and opinions to help the system flow naturally.

Actions

- Where is your organisation now on its journey to creating a coaching culture?

- Look for opportunities where you can start to develop a coaching culture.

- What can you do to role-model a coaching leadership style?

- Decide what support you need in developing a coaching culture.

- What one action can you take today to develop a coaching culture?

Amy's actions

Action notes from coaching session

Creating a coaching culture

I need to make sure I am role-modelling a coaching leadership style at all times.

I need to work with a professional training partner to ensure we create a robust coaching framework that we can roll out into the business.

I need to support my team to develop their coaching skills with their own teams.

I need to gain buy-in from the Board so that we can invest in the culture change programme alongside the operational transformation programme.

I need to coach the system.

Conclusion

Amy had been in her role for two years. The coaching culture programme had not been without its implementation problems, but her transparent and vulnerable leadership style was exuding confidence and the Board trusted her. Amy had reluctantly agreed to stop seeing her coach and had learned to effectively self-coach and coach her team. She had also started working with a mentor who was ten years older than her and had made a successful transition from COO to CEO in another organisation.

Amy was having lunch with her mentor and they were discussing how she felt the interview for the Fortune Industries CEO position had gone the week before. 'It's been a long journey, and it all started with a tough question from my coach,' she said reflectively. 'What was the question?' her mentor asked curiously. 'Who are you?' Amy replied. Just then, her mobile phone rang. It was the call she had been waiting for. Amy listened intently for what seemed an eternity and then replied, 'Yes. I would be honoured.' Her mentor smiled and said, 'Well, Amy, who are you?' Amy paused and beamed. 'I am the new CEO of Fortune Industries!' As she replied, Amy knew her self-coaching cycle was about to begin again.

Amy's journey to becoming a CEO through the support of a coach and others around her is fairly typical. Unfortunately, most leaders in a new role tend to focus on their teams first. They try to fix them or get them to change their ways. Hopefully this book has demonstrated that fulfilling your potential as a leader has to start with you and not your team.

The self-coaching cycle

The self-coaching cycle begins every time you rediscover the latest version of who you are. When Amy joined Fortune Industries, she was like a fish out of water. Nothing was familiar anymore. She discovered that, with the support of her coach, she could Reconnect with who she was and why she was there. She could Refocus on what was truly important for her to do every minute of the day. She could Regenerate into an Amy that was fulfilling more potential by practising self-coaching and leading herself more effectively. When Amy eventually gained the CEO position, she needed to Reconnect with who she had become and not who she was when she'd started as COO.

Not every leader has the opportunity to work with an executive coach, but for those that do (or have in the past), I encourage you to Reconnect with what you learned during that time and with the information in this book to work out where you are in your self-coaching cycle at this stage in your life. Practise the self-coaching techniques in the relevant chapters and be kind to yourself as you try and incorporate them into your everyday lives.

For those that have not worked with a coach before and will not get the opportunity any time soon, I encourage you to re-read this book from time to time to jog your memory about which chapters can be of help as you attempt to self-coach in realising your potential. Self-coaching is hard work. Always ask for support from your friends, family and colleagues as you practise the twelve disciplines. The diagram and summary below reference how you might be feeling in the different parts of the self-coaching cycle.

The Self-coaching Cycle

Reconnect

Self-leadership

Many leaders need to start here in the self-coaching cycle, especially those who feel that they are not in control of their own future. They tend to blame others for bad outcomes. They can come across as victimised or having a lot of bad luck all at once. They tend to find it difficult to hold themselves to account and have poor discipline in relation to their own wellbeing.

Who am I?

Many leaders start here when they feel lost in life and know deep down that they are being shaped by their organisation in a way that feels uncomfortable. They tend to come to work wearing a mask that conceals their true feelings and who they really are. They tend to have lost sight of who they really are. Leaders who start here can be sad, depressed or have feelings of hopelessness.

Why am I here?

Many leaders start here when they start to question their futures in their organisations. There is a lack of alignment between their own needs in life and what the organisations need from them. Many leaders who start here instinctively know that they can't pursue their core values in their current role. Something is missing, but they don't know what. Some leaders can't clearly articulate their purpose.

Emotional intelligence

Leaders who start here might have received some feedback from others that surprised them. It may be that they have started to upset others and don't know why. Some leaders may realise that they have been focusing on 'I' rather than 'we' in relationships for too long. Many leaders who start here don't have much understanding of what others think about them. They rarely ask for feedback.

Refocus

What is essential?

Leaders start here when they have not got enough time in the day and never get to the end of their to-do lists. They spread themselves too thinly across a wide range of tasks and they find delegation challenging. They don't have clarity on what is important to spend time on and they tend to be reactive to events around them. They never find enough time for building strong, trust-based relationships.

Trust

Leaders who start here don't know what their stakeholders think of them. They find it hard to trust other people and they don't tend to be vulnerable with people they think may judge them. They tend to withhold information from teams and are not completely transparent with their stakeholders. Some leaders don't trust themselves to deliver against certain objectives and create barriers to stop others getting too close to them.

Accountability

Leaders who start here would sometimes describe themselves as 'coasters'. They just do enough to meet their objectives as nobody else is holding them accountable for their actions. They feel they can get away with cutting corners and that they are skillful in managing their stakeholders, even though they don't really know what they think of them. They tend to avoid conflict and are not skilled in performance management.

Creating space

Leaders who start here tend to bounce from meeting to meeting and are proud to be known as 'great operators'. They tend to feel good about themselves when they are doing rather than being or thinking. These leaders warmly talk about their open-door policy, but those that enter their office for a chat feel the time they have together is superficial and transactional rather than deep and meaningful.

Regenerate

Resilience

Leaders who start here might be feeling stressed and exhausted. They have decided to put others first and have not focused on their own wellbeing. They feel that they are not as agile as they need to be and rarely feel in flow. The day can go slowly and the leader might find it difficult to maintain their energy levels. The leader will often state that they are coping and that they just need to get through the next few days and then things will get better.

Mental fitness

Leaders who start here might have noticed that their negative thoughts are becoming more dominant. They might be judgmental of others and make key decisions from a position of negativity. Some leaders become aware of their self-limiting beliefs and how they are getting in the way of career progression. Others tend to be easily triggered by negative behaviour from key stakeholders, which then damages the relationship further.

Leading teams

Leaders who start here tend to have focused on their own personal development and have forgotten to invest in their team and their function. They are skilled in self-leadership and other self-coaching techniques and recognise that they need to demand more of their team. They tend to have insufficient support from HR so they state that team development is next on the agenda, but delay the investment until there is more stability in the team and end up focusing on themselves again.

Coaching culture

Leaders who start here have been through the whole self-coaching cycle and have experienced the benefits personally and professionally. They are authentic leaders who create powerful visions for their organisations and recognise that the best way to realise the whole potential of all their employees is in creating a coaching culture. They role-model a coaching leadership style and are known for being great listeners.

I have worked with hundreds of leaders across a variety of cultures, and in my experience, those that embrace and live the self-coaching disciplines in this book tend to be happier and more successful in their professional careers. After you have read the book, the next step is to begin your life-long journey of self-leadership and self-coaching. You will become clearer about what your personal and professional dreams are and feel motivated and confident that you can start to work towards those dreams.

In the new world that we find ourselves in, there has probably never been a better time to reclaim your personal and professional dreams. Best of luck on your own personal journey. I would be interested to hear your own personal stories and I am always open to feedback on my thoughts and techniques in this book.

Visit www.tallents-partnership.com for more information. You can access more resources linked to this book and about self-coaching at www.selfcoachingforleaders.com

Resources

These books have been useful in developing the ideas and techniques that support my daily self-coaching practice. You may find some of them interesting as you continue on your own personal journey.

Little Wins: The huge power of thinking like a toddler by Paul Lindley (Penguin, 2017)

Finding Your Own North Star: How to claim the life you were meant to live by Martha Beck (Piatkus, 2003)

Leadership from the Inside Out: Becoming a leader for life by Kevin Cashman (Berrett-Koehler Publishers, 2008)

What Got You Here Won't Get You There: How successful people become even more successful by Marshall Goldsmith (Profile Books, 2008)

The 4 Stages of Psychological Safety: Defining the path to inclusion and innovation by Tim Clark (Berrett-Koehler Publishers, 2020)

Presence: How to use positive energy for success in every situation by Patsy Rodenburg (Penguin, 2009)

Dare to Lead: Brave work. Tough conversations. Whole hearts by Brené Brown (Vermilion, 2018)

Emotional Intelligence: Why it can matter more than IQ by Daniel Goleman (Bloomsbury Publishing, 1996)

The Culture Code: The secrets of highly successful groups by Daniel Coyle (Generic Publishing, 2019)

Self-leadership and the One Minute Manager: Discuss the magic of no excuses! by Ken Blanchard, Susan Fowler et al (HarperCollins, 2006)

Acknowledgements

I would like to thank all of the leaders I have worked with over the last twenty-five years. You have been an endless source of inspiration. Thank you for letting me into your worlds and challenging your ways of being. It takes great courage to work with a coach. I admire all those that have jumped into the unknown with curiosity and beginners' minds.

I would also like to thank all of my work colleagues from over the last thirty years for teaching me many things about teamwork and ambition.

Special thanks to my amazing coach supervisor, Elle Harrison. We had an incredible twelve-month journey together.

Thank you to all the faculty members and fellow students from the AOEC's Practitioner Diploma Course (PD94) in London. You inspired me to be adventurous and to explore who I really am.

Thanks to Vanda, Richard, Andrew, Tim, Darren, Alistair, Vicky, Nigel, Jack and Melissa for kindly reviewing the book and suggesting improvements before it was sent for professional editing.

Thank you to the team at Rethink Press for coaching, supporting and professionally publishing my first book. I couldn't have done it without you.

Finally, thank you to Ollie, our three-year-old Cavapoo, for reminding me of the importance of presence and unconditional love every minute of the day.

The Author

Andrew Tallents has over twenty-five years' experience in delivering a wide range of leadership consulting solutions to a variety of organisations around the world. He grew up on a council estate in Manchester, and after graduating from Salford University with a business degree, he joined the utility industry and spent his early career in business support functions.

He then moved into the recruitment industry where he supported CEOs in growing their organisations and developing their own careers. During this time, he was fortunate to work with global organisations and developed his multicultural awareness, enabling him to work with a wide variety of leadership styles.

He established the Tallents Partnership in 2017 to support leaders who are ambitious for themselves and their organisations. He has worked with large corporate organisations and small not-for-profit organisations and has learned that in any organisation, a leader is only as successful as the relationships they create and develop.

Andrew is proud of his family and circle of friends and associates. When he is not supporting his clients, he enjoys working towards fulfilling his potential on the golf course. He also supports charities in the social mobility sector. Andrew lives in the Wirral in the UK with his wife, children and Ollie the Cavapoo.

Andrew can be contacted at:

🌐 www.tallents-partnership.com

💼 www.linkedin.com/in/theleadershipcoach

🐦 @atallents